The H.P.A. Parents Association
will use the proceeds
from the sales of KAMAKANI COOKS
to support the growth and development
of Hawaii Preparatory Academy.

For additional copies, use the order form
at the back of the book or write:
KAMAKANI COOKS
c/o H.P.A. Parents Association
P.O.Box 428
Kamuela, Hawaii 96743

Graphic Layout & Design By:
Studio M Design, DeWayne Sluss
Kailua-Kona, Hawaii

ISBN#0-9638082-0-6

First Printing October, 1993

Printed by: Heritage Graphics &
Everbest Printing, Hong Kong

KAMAKANI
COOKS

Winning
Big Island Recipes
from
Students, Parents, Teachers,
Alumnae and Friends
of
Hawaii Preparatory Academy

SPECIAL THANKS TO

All the incredible cooks who have donated recipes; we wish we could have used them all. We thank everyone who took the time to share their favorites, from "Baked Potato a la Dumpe" by Jim Moore '70, the Class of '64 Kalua Pig by Peter W. Cannon, to Rick Habein's "Elephant Stew" (Class of '78) and Franz Solmssen's "Kaluamakani Delight". ("This recipe cannot be made without horses; you need the horses to transport the *ingredements* to a remote location." F.S.) Naturally, with help of this caliber, the job of the Cookbook Committee was a breeze.

THE COOKBOOK COMMITTEE
Niki Clark Chairperson
Joan Anderson • Glen Budge
Heather Cole • Kadie Harris
Marty Hind • Lizika Lam
Candace Peterson • Brigitte Rutgers

A round of applause for these dedicated ladies who sacrificed their diets, their lunch hours, and their sanity to create this cookbook. They investigated new recipes, dug out old favorites, taste-tested alumnae specials and met monthly to sample promising entries. After thoughtful discussion on the merits of each item ("My husband would never eat this!"), the committee voted to include the spectacular and eliminate the ho-hum. (All Velveeta cheese concoctions were OUT.)

Special thanks to Chairperson, Niki Clark, whose time, energy, typing skills, persistence and terrific taste buds, have brought this three year project to a happy end. Without Niki, this labor of love would be, as the Australians like to say, "down the gurgle".

Special thanks to Kadie Harris whose well known flair in graphic design and layout has transformed a hopeless heap of typewritten pages into an elegant and pleasing book. The committee cannot thank Kadie enough for picking up the pieces, preparing them for the printer, and charging forward to meet the dreaded deadlines!

Special thanks to Maile Melrose for the history of Hawaii Preparatory Academy and the history of Waimea.

SPECIAL THANKS TO
THE FOLLOWING CONTRIBUTORS

Harry Achilles
Mr & Mrs. A.D. Ackerman
Dixie Adams
Joan Anderson
LeBerta Atherton
Roberta H. Barlow
Benjamin Bennett
Melinda Bollinger
Dodie Borho
Patsy J. Bowers
Mebane Boyd
Kathleen Brilhante
Balbi Brooks
Randy Brown
Bill & Anne Brye
Glen Budge
Mrs. Ward Buscher
Elna Calder
John F. Campbell
Charlotte Champlin
Peter Cannon
Gloria Chapman
Charles Chidiac
Sue E. Ching
Rona Chumbook
Laura Clagstone
Lisa Clark
Niki Clark
Heather Cole
JoAnn Conley
Dean A. Covey
Suzanne Clough
Annie Cowles
Wendy Craven
Susan Detwiler
Jane Dierenfield
Michael O. Donnelly
Leslie Dunbar
Dee Dwyer
Martha and Kate English
Ken Fischer
Kathlyn Furuya
Tracy Goodman-Zotti
Mrs. Henry Greenwell
Pat Greenwell
Rick Habein
Caroline Hagen
Kadie Harris
Marc Hasegawa
Matthew Hasegawa
Margaret Hecht

Jamsie Herbert
Marty Hind
Jennifer Hindle
Joan A. Hutchinson
Barbara Jacobson
Midge Jambor
Bill and Cathie Jardine
Kathi Johnson
Margie Judd
Louise B. Kenar
Margie Kiessling
Carol Kindt
Mrs. Garfield King
Larry Klingman
Mrs. Robert Knutson
Juliette Koning
Lizika Lam
Nancy MacGregor
Ty & Leah Mackey
Martha Maglothin
Patricia Maglothin
Sean Magoun
Marisa and Suliana Manley
Douglas and Melinda Mannen
Nancy Lee Markham
Julie Mattson
Cory Lynn McCullough
Nancy McGonegal
Helen McQuaid
L. Mecca
Jim Moore
Anne Murtha-Powell
Kevin Nakamaru
Mrs. Ruzica Negovetic
Thomas Noyes
Michael O'Donnelly
Wendy O'Leary
Colleen O'Malley
Kathy Okumoto-Miller
Lana Olmstead
Susan Damron Opperman
Todd Atherton Perkins
Candace Peterson
Dianne Pickens
Jo Piltz
Mel Pobre
Beth Podol
Edward Podol
Carol Povey
Diana Quaintance
Cassie & Jill Quaintance

Jadelyn Ramos
Kitty Rathe-Iwamoto
Shirley Rae
Janice Rearden
Jerry & Sue Reynolds
Phyllis Richards
Mrs. Leone Rolf
Jada Rufo
Brigitte & Nick Rutgers
Susan K. Ruuwe
Jean Salmon
Mrs. Rowe Sanderson
Elizabeth Schilling
Lila Hasegawa Scott
Becky Phillips Sleeman
Sharon and Dick Solmssen
Linda Startsman
Mrs. Q. M. Stephen-Hassard
Nona Hasegawa Tagliavento
Viviene Tooman
Robert Tully
Hideko Usami
Pauline Ventura*
Beverly Warns
Kate Weight
Mildred Weight
Sandy Weinrich
Nancy J.P. Witt
Margaret Woodard
Ruth Young
The Canoe House
Tres Hombres

&
ARTISTS

Guy Buffet
Janice Gail
Martha Greenwell
Pat Hall
Kadie Harris
Clem Lam
Kathy Long
Miles Mason
Candace Peterson
Marcia Ray
Jane Thronas
Loretta Viecelli
Harry Wishard

HAWAII PREPARATORY ACADEMY

In 1949, Bishop Harry S. Kennedy founded the Hawaii Episcopal Academy as a boarding school for boys in grades 7 through 12 in Waimea. The campus was on the grounds of St. James Episcopal Church and the school buildings were actually temporary classrooms built by the Sea Bees during World War II for Waimea School. School enrollment included 23 students.

In 1954, James Monroe Taylor was appointed headmaster of the fledgling school. Fresh from the ivy covered walls of Choate, he spent the next 20 years instilling discipline, respect, and the value of an education into his faculty and students.

In 1957, the Episcopal Church surrendered its direction of the school to a new governing board and Hawaii Preparatory Academy was born. The next year saw the purchase of 55 acres of land from the Territory of Hawaii, and well known Honolulu architect, Vladimir Ossipoff, set to work designing the campus. In September of 1958, Lynn Taylor founded "The Little School" to educate elementary aged children. For a few hectic years, HPA existed in two places, with students being bussed to and from St. James and the new campus. All that ended in 1963 with grades 7-12 firmly established at the "Upper Campus" and the elementary classes remaining at St. James Church grounds.

The 1960's were years of tremendous growth - new teachers, more construction on campus, landscaping galore, and an enlarging student body. The Fall of 1970 saw the arrival of 29 girl boarders! HPA became a co-ed boarding school overnight. The Taylors retired in 1974, knowing HPA would go forward under the leadership of Edson P. Sheppard, Jr. In 1976, Woodson "Woody" Woods gave the buildings of the Waimea Village Inn to the school, leading to the opening of the Village Campus for grades 1-8. The first kindergarten class was added in 1980, taught by Headmaster Ron Tooman's wife, Vivienne.

The 1980's saw the addition of the Kona Campus for grades K-5 at Kainaliu and Puuloa. Back in Waimea, the Upper Campus gained a new look with the gift of 20 acres of adjoining land from Richard Smart, the addition of Waimea's first swimming pool in 1989, and the ground breaking for a new performing arts center.

Nearly 45 years have passed since HPA's damp and dogged beginning. Although much has changed, many things endure. Headmaster John Colson will have to remind the freshman class "to get the dirt out of your eyes" sooner or later. The faculty still sit down to dinner with boarders, gently reminding them not to slurp their soup. Athletes still side-step assorted obstacles as they charge through the rolling pastures in search of strength and prowess. The infamous wind - Kamakani - still knocks unwary newcomers off balance, shredding homework, hairdos and self-confidence in the process. Like Waimea's trees, HPA's aspiring sons and daughters must learn to diplomatically bend and send down deep roots.

UP COUNTRY WAIMEA

"Waimea" means "reddish water" in Hawaiian. For most of the 20th century, tidy Waimea housewives cursed that water which frustrated all attempts to have gleaming white bathrooms and snowy white linen. However, Waimea's red waters proved to be the source of her health, wealth and happiness.

Long before Captain James Cook bumped into these islands in 1778, Hawaii's gardeners built stone walls and channeled stream waters into terraced patches of taro and sweet potatoes.

When Captain George Vancouver first hiked to the green pastures of Waimea in 1794, surprise and delight surely filled his heart. Not only had he found a happy home for his seasick cattle, but what a spot for growing those vegetables so dear to an Englishman's heart - Irish potatoes, peas, beans, cabbage and carrots!

Under royal Kapu, great herds of Mexican longhorns roamed the hillsides, trampling the vegetation and goring unwary travelers. Horses were landed at Kawaihae in 1803 and soon also ran wild in the foothills of Mauna Kea. In 1815, Kamehameha I hired an ex-seaman from Massachusetts, John Palmer Parker, the founder of Parker Ranch, to kill the horned intruders.

Change came fast and furious. In 1820, the first missionaries arrived. Whalers used the islands as a winter retreat. Foreigners flocked to Hawaii's shores demanding ever increasing amounts of food, grog, timber and firewood! As loads of hides, tallow and salt meat were hauled from Waimea to Kawaihae, the upland village acquired a bustling commercial air.

Desperate to solve the cattle mess, King Kamehameha III imported three Mexican vaqueros to teach Hawaiians how to ride horseback and tame cattle. Father Lorenzo Lyons came to Waimea in 1832 and remained until his death in 1886. Makua Laiana's gifts to Waimea's people still shine - beautiful Imiola Church and "Hawaii Aloha", his heartfelt song of love for the place he came to call home.

Members of the Hawaiian royal court frequently visited Waimea and Mana, lending an air of romance to the town's reputation. After 1900, Parker Ranch became known for its prize cattle, fleet race horses and sheep.

Cattle and ranching formed the backbone of this town for well over 150 years. That began to change when Laurence Rockefeller first spied Kauna'oa Bay, the site of the Mauna Kea Beach Hotel. The fate of South Kohala was sealed.

Now, as the era of plantation life draws to a close in neighboring communities, Waimea continues to grow to suit an unknown future. Generous benefactors, such as the late Lucy Henriques and Richard Smart, have supported not only the town's basic needs, but have enhanced our future with a performing arts theatre, private schools and a state of the art medical center. Mauna Kea still stands blue and serene, the same kamakani blows, the same rains drift across the sky, and the streams flow to the sea. The color of the water is red.

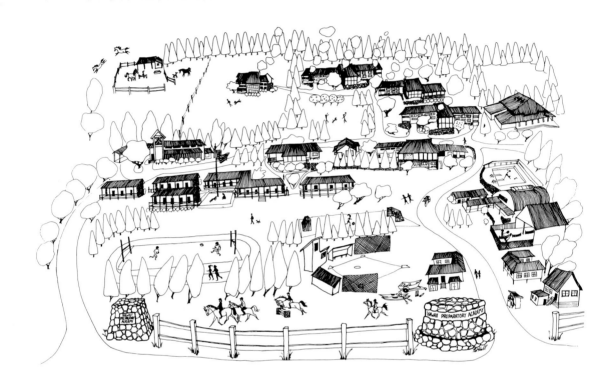

HAWAII PREPARATORY ACADEMY
By Pat Hall

Pat Hall has been a professional artist in Hawaii for over twenty-five years. Known for her watercolor and acrylic paintings, as well as many fanciful drawings, she is comfortable working in a variety of media including wood sculpture, clay, pen and ink, block printing and etching. Pat has illustrated a number of books and has her own line of greeting card designs. Originally from Balboa Island in California, Pat now lives in Waimea with her husband, Howard. She divides her time between their three children, two grandchildren, numerous pets, a small farm and her artwork.

CONTENTS

EARLY MOON, WAIMEA
By Miles Mason

Originally from California, Miles Mason moved to the Big Island in 1987. Being red-green colorblind, Miles' artistic development began in black and white. His early works were elaborately stippled pen and ink studies of shells collected on his travels abroad. Experimentation with non-traditional uses of watercolor led him to develop an innovative style of layering and stippling in his paintings, the result being an intensity of color not usually associated with the watercolor medium. His striking images have been acclaimed by art critics, won numerous prizes at juried shows, and have attracted a growing number of eager collectors.

PUPUS (APPETIZERS)

APRICOT BRIE

ASPARAGUS SPEARS

CAPONATA

CHICKEN & JALAPENO NACHOS

EGGPLANT DIP WITH GARLIC

HAWAIIAN SALSA

SUN DRIED TOMATO TORTE

TIROPETES

TROPICAL LUMPIA

JAY'S NON-FAT BLACK BEANS

SPARKLING SANGRIA

KAHUA ICED TEA

APRICOT BRIE

Phyllo dough
Brie
Apricot preserves

1 Preheat oven to 350 degrees.

2 Layer six sheets of phyllo on baking sheet (stagger layers to create a circle), brushing each layer with melted butter. Place Brie in center of phyllo and spread with apricot preserves on sides and top. Fold phyllo up and around the cheese.

3 Cover top of cheese with six sheets of phyllo, again staggering layers and brushing each with melted butter. Smooth top and sides. Tuck ends under Brie. Brush top and sides with butter. Bake for 20-30 minutes or until golden brown. Let stand for 30-45 minutes before serving. Cut into small wedges. Serve with crackers.

ASPARAGUS SPEARS

1 Preheat oven to 400 degrees. Bake garlic cloves by placing in small baking dish, drizzle with olive oil, then toss to coat. Bake until garlic is very soft (about 15 minutes). Remove garlic from oil, cool and peel. Add garlic, goat cheese and pepper to oil and mash together.

2 Cook asparagus in large pot of boiling, salted water until crisp, tender (about 5 minutes). Cool by placing spears in bowl of ice water. Drain and pat dry.

3 Cut prosciutto in half lengthwise. Spread one side of each piece with cheese mixture. Place one asparagus spear at the short end of prosciutto and roll up tightly. Transfer to cookie sheet.

4 These can be prepared one day ahead - just cover tightly and refrigerate.

5 When ready to serve, preheat for about 5 minutes in 400 degree oven, or if desired, can be served chilled.

*2 cloves garlic
  (unpeeled)
1 tablespoon olive oil
2-1/2 ounces mild
  goat cheese
1/4 teaspoon pepper
30 asparagus spears
15 paper thin slices
  prosciutto*

CAPONATA

1 medium eggplant,
  do not peel
1/2 cup olive oil
2 tablespoons olive oil
1 large onion, finely
  chopped
2 cups celery, thinly
  sliced
1 green or red pepper,
  finely chopped
1/3 cup vinegar, mild
  like tarragon
2 teaspoons sugar
1 clove garlic, mashed
3 tablespoons tomato
  paste, mixed with 1/2
  cup water
1 tablespoon parsley,
  chopped
1/2 cup sliced pimento
  stuffed olives
1/3 cup capers
Salt and pepper

1 Dice eggplant into cubes about 1/2 inch thick. Sauté in 1/2 cup olive oil for 10 to 15 minutes. Stir frequently. Remove eggplant, add remaining 2 tablespoons olive oil and sauté onion for several minutes. Add the celery and the green or red pepper, and sauté for 4 or 5 minutes. Add remaining ingredients, stir thoroughly, cover and simmer over very low heat for about 10 minutes. Season to taste with salt and pepper. Serve chilled with sesame crackers or thinly sliced French bread.

Serves 10 - 16 persons.

CHICKEN & JALAPENO NACHOS

1 Preheat oven to 375 degrees.

2 Combine chicken, cream cheese, jalapeno peppers, onion, garlic, cumin, chili powder and grated cheese in a large bowl. Beat with a mixer until blended. Season to taste with salt and pepper.

3 Spread each pita round with a generous portion of filling. Place on cookie sheet and bake until puffed and bubbling (5-7 minutes). Immediately cut into wedges and serve in a napkin-lined basket.

1 whole chicken breast, poached, skinned, boned and diced

12 ounce cream cheese, room temperature

2 jalapeno peppers, seeded and minced

3 tablespoons chopped red onion

2 cloves garlic, minced

1 teaspoon ground cumin

1 teaspoon chili powder

1-1/2 cups grated Monterey Jack cheese

Salt and pepper, to taste

6 medium size pita, each cut & separated into 2 rounds.

EGGPLANT DIP WITH GARLIC

2 large eggplants
2 large garlic cloves
4 tablespoons oil
2 tablespoons fresh
  lemon juice
2 tablespoons fresh
  oregano
1 teaspoon ground
  cumin

1 Preheat oven to 450 degrees. Cut slits in eggplants with tip of knife and insert garlic sliver into each slit. Place eggplants in baking pan and bake until very tender, about 1 hour. Cut each eggplant in half and cool slightly.

2 Scrape eggplant pulp from skin into colander and let drain. Transfer eggplant to processor. Add oil, lemon juice, 2 tablespoons oregano and cumin. Purée until smooth. Season with salt and pepper. Cool completely. (Can be prepared one day ahead). Cover and refrigerate.

3 To serve: Line a serving platter with lettuce leaves and tomato slices. Mound eggplant mixture in center. Serve with pita cut into wedges, jicama slices, or other crudites.

HAWAIIAN SALSA

1 Skin and quarter onions. Seed and quarter all peppers. Chop medium to fine in food processor. Combine in a mixing bowl, then add white pepper, cayenne pepper and tabasco.

2 Core, quarter and chop tomatoes in food processor and add to above mixture.

3 Combine parsley and cilantro in food processor. Chop medium to fine and add to mixture. Dice papaya and add to mixture. Add soy sauce and lemon juice. Mix well.

4 Taste and if too sour, add 2 tablespoons of brown sugar.

5 Chill in refrigerator.

6 *Maui onions*
2 *yellow peppers*
2 *red peppers*
3 *medium Anaheim peppers*
6 *large tomatoes*
1/2 *bunch cilantro*
1/2 *bunch parsley*
2 *lemons or limes*
2 *teaspoons tabasco sauce*
3 *tablespoons soy sauce*
2 *teaspoons white pepper*
2 *teaspoons cayenne pepper*
1 *strawberry papaya*
2 *tablespoons brown sugar (optional)*

SUN DRIED TOMATO TORTE

1 pound cream cheese
1 pound butter
1/4 cup pesto (may be
  commercially bought)
8 dried tomatoes

1 Bring cream cheese and butter to room temperature, cream together and divide into thirds.

2 Blend pesto and tomatoes together in food processor, and divide in half.

3 Line a quart bowl or mold with wet cheese cloth and layer cheese-butter mixture and pesto-tomato mixture. Repeat layers ending with cheese-butter mixture on top.

4 Unmold and serve with crackers.

TIROPETES

1 Thoroughly combine cheeses, eggs and pepper. Cut pastry sheets lengthwise into fifths. Work with one strip at a time, being sure to keep remaining dough moist by covering with damp cloth. Brush each strip with melted butter. Place a rounded teaspoon of cheese filling on bottom end of strip. Fold over the corner to cover the filling and to make a triangle shape. Continue folding like folding a flag to end of strip. Place triangles on baking sheet and bake in a 350 degree oven 20 minutes or until golden. Serve warm or cold.

Note: *To freeze before baking, place in a box or container with a double fold of waxed paper between each layer. They may be thawed or baked frozen allowing extra baking time if frozen.*

1 pound feta cheese, crumbled
6 ounces cottage cheese
3 eggs, beaten
Dash of pepper
1 pound phyllo dough, thawed
1/2 pound butter, melted

TROPICAL LUMPIA

1 large clove garlic
Juice of 1 lime
1/2 cup chopped pickled
  Maui onions
1 tablespoon chopped
  red jalapeno chiles
20 lumpia wrappers
8 ounces Brie cheese,
  thinly sliced into 20
  pieces
2 mangoes, peeled and
  diced
1/4 cup unsalted butter
1/4 cup safflower oil
  sweet and sour sauce
  (optional)

1 Cook garlic and lime juice for 2-3 minutes until liquid is gone. Take off heat, add chopped onion and chiles.

2 On each wrapper put about 1/2 tablespoon onion/chile mixture, 1 tablespoon mango and 1 slice cheese. Roll up as illustrated on lumpia package. Brush all over with mixture of butter and oil. Place on cookie sheet. (Can be prepared to this point, one day in advance and refrigerated.) Bring to room temperature and bake for 5 minutes in a preheated 475 degrees oven. Serve with sauce if desired.

SWEET & SOUR SAUCE

1/2 cup sugar
1/2 cup water
1/8 cup (2 tablespoons)
  liquid from pickled
  onions
1/8 cup vinegar
1 clove garlic, crushed
1 teaspoon chopped red
  jalapeno peppers
1/2 teaspoon salt

1 Combine sugar and water in sauce pan and cook over medium heat for about 10 minutes, until consistency of syrup. Remove from heat. Add the rest of ingredients and mix well.

JAY'S NON-FAT BLACK BEANS

Great served cold as a spread - even better the next day!

1 Soak beans overnight. Drain. Bring to a boil in 6 cups water. Reduce heat and simmer 1-1/2 to 2 hours.

2 Sauté carrots, onions and spices in a little water until tender. Add to the beans with the honey and simmer for another 45 minutes.

1-16 ounce bag black beans
4 large carrots, grated
1 large onion, grated
6 cups water
1 teaspoon salt
1 tablespoon chili pepper
1 teaspoon garlic powder
2 tablespoons honey

SPARKLING SANGRIA

2 medium oranges
1 medium lemon
1/4 cup sugar
1/4 teaspoon
  cinnamon
1-6 ounce can frozen
  apple juice
1-25.4 ounce bottle
  sparkling apple cider
  (well chilled)
2 cups (or more)
  sparkling water

This non-alcoholic beverage is festive for luncheons.

1 Squeeze and reserve juice from 1 orange and 1 lemon. Cut second orange and lemon into thin slices.

2 Place orange and lemon slices in bottom of large pitcher. Sprinkle with sugar and cinnamon. Crush the fruit and sugar with long spoon. Blend in reserved citrus juice and apple juice concentrate. Stir in apple cider. Add sparkling water to taste.

Serve. Makes 2 quarts.

KAHUA ICED TEA

1 Steep tea with mint sprigs until twice as strong as normal. Remove bags only.

2 In another pot bring to a boil, sugar and 1-1/2 cups water. Add sugar mixture to tea. Add an additional 2 quarts of water. Add lemon juice when cooled otherwise lemons will be bitter.

This will keep in the refrigator for 2-3 weeks. Makes approximately 1 gallon.

6 Lipton tea bags
4 sprigs fresh mint
2 quarts boiling water
1-1/2 cups sugar
1-1/2 cups water
5 lemons - juiced or
10 tablespoons
  lemon juice

ENTRANCE TO H.P.A.
By Martha Greenwell

Martha Greenwell was born and raised in Hawaii. She was introduced to the joys of drawing and oil painting at an early age by her father, Sherwood M. Lowrey, who was himself a talented artist. Her husband, James M. Greenwell was on the H.P.A. board and served as chairman for five years. Their son, James S. Greenwell, and two grandchildren, Britt and Heather Craven, are H.P.A. graduates.

SALADS & DRESSINGS

ALAPAKI'S KASHI & BEAN SALAD

BEAN SPROUT SALAD

BILL'S CREOLE COLESLAW

CHINESE CHICKEN SALAD

JACKSON SALAD

ORIENTAL CABBAGE SALAD

HOT POTATO SALAD

IRISH MIST SALAD DRESSING

PAPAYA SEED DRESSING

VINAIGRETTE SALAD DRESSING

ALAPAKI'S KASHI & BEAN SALAD

1 cup kashi and/or
   brown rice
   combination, cooked
1 pound can kidney
   beans
2 eggs, hard cooked and
   chopped
1/4 cup onion, chopped
1/4 cup celery, chopped
1/4 cup red, yellow, or
   green bell pepper,
   chopped
1/2 cup sweet pickle
   relish
1/2 teaspoon salt
1/4 teaspoon pepper
1/3 cup mayonnaise
1 teaspoon vinegar

1 Combine kidney beans with rice, eggs, onion, celery, bell pepper and relish. Blend salt, pepper, mayonnaise and vinegar. Mix lightly with salad. Chill.

Serves 6.

BEAN SPROUT SALAD

1 Pour boiling water over bean sprouts in a colander. Rinse with cold water. Add onions, tomato, soy sauce, oil, salt and pepper. Refrigerate.

Serves 4.

1 package bean sprouts
4 green onions with
  leaves, chopped
1 large tomato, chopped
2 tablespoons soy sauce
1 teaspoon sesame oil
Salt and pepper to taste

BILL'S CREOLE COLESLAW

1 Chop cabbage into 1" chunks. Do not shred. Mix sauce in a separate container and pour over cabbage. Toss and Serve.

1/2 tablespoon garlic
  powder
1/2 tablespoon ground
  black pepper
7 ounces Zatarains
  mustard or Dijon
2-1/2 cups mayonnaise
5 ounces red wine
  vinegar
5 ounces olive oil
2 large heads of fresh
  Waimea cabbage

CHINESE CHICKEN SALAD

2 or 3 cups cooked
  chicken, shredded
1 head lettuce, torn
1 head won bok
  (Chinese cabbage),
  chopped
3 stalks celery, sliced
3 stalks green onion,
  chopped
1 bunch Chinese
  parsley, finely
  chopped
1 package won ton
  chips, crushed
1/2 cup dry roasted
  peanuts

1 Mix all salad ingredients in bowl. Sprinkle with dressing and toss. Serve immediately.

ORIENTAL SALAD DRESSING

2 tablespoons Hoisin
  sauce
4 tablespoons catsup
2 tablespoons sesame
  oil
4 tablespoons vegetable
  oil
2 tablespoons vinegar
  or lemon juice
4 tablespoons sugar
1 teaspoon salt

1 Mix all ingredients in a container. Serve immediately.

JACKSON SALAD

1 Purée onion with vinegar in blender. Transfer to medium bowl. Using electric mixer blend in mustard, sugar, salt and pepper. Gradually add oil in thin, steady stream and continue beating until thick.

2 Cook bacon in skillet on medium heat until crisp. Drain on paper towel. Cool completely. Crumble.

3 Mix lettuce, hearts of palm, artichoke hearts, cheese, and bacon in serving bowl. Toss with dressing to taste and serve.

1/4 onion, chopped
3 tablespoons cider vinegar
2 teaspoons spicy brown mustard
1/2 teaspoon sugar
1/2 teaspoon salt
1/4 teaspoon fresh ground black pepper
1 cup vegetable oil
1/2 pound bacon
2 bunches romaine lettuce, torn into bite size pieces
1-7.5 ounce can hearts of palm, drained and quartered
1-8.5 ounce can water packed artichoke hearts, drained and quartered
4 ounces blue cheese, crumbled

ORIENTAL CABBAGE SALAD

1/2 head cabbage,
  grated
4 to 8 green onions,
  sliced thin
5 to 10 mushrooms,
  sliced thin
1/2 cup slivered
  almonds, toasted
1 tablespoon sesame
  seeds, toasted
1/2 package ramen
  noodles, uncooked &
  broken

1 Toss all ingredients together with dressing just before serving.

DRESSING

1/4 cup sesame seeds,
  lightly toasted
2/3 cup salad oil
  (peanut or vegetable)
2 tablespoons lemon
  juice
2 tablespoons rice wine
  vinegar
2 tablespoons brown
  sugar
1 clove garlic, minced
1 tablespoon soy sauce
1/4 teaspoon salt

1 Dressing is best when made a few hours ahead of time.

HOT POTATO SALAD

1 Cook bacon, onions and green pepper together. Drain on paper towel. Mix mustard, mayonnaise, sugar, salt and pepper. Mix with potatoes in large bowl. Stir in bacon, onion, and green pepper mixture.

1/2 pound bacon, diced
3/4 cup onion, chopped
1/3 cup green pepper, chopped
6 cups boiled potatoes, diced
3/4 cup mayonnaise
1/4 cup mustard
1/4 cup sugar
1 teaspoon salt
1/4 teaspoon pepper

IRISH MIST SALAD DRESSING

1/4 cup Dijon mustard
1/4 cup Irish Mist liqueur
3 tablespoons red wine
   vinegar
3 tablespoons honey
6 tablespoons vegetable
   oil
Salt and freshly ground
   white pepper (optional)

1 Blend mustard, liqueur, vinegar and honey in small bowl. Whisk in oil in thin stream (can be prepared in food processor). Season with salt and pepper. Refrigerate.

This is delicious on a salad made with spinach, red onions, sliced strawberries and kiwi fruit.

PAPAYA SEED DRESSING

1/4 cup tarragon
   vinegar
1/4 cup sugar
1/4 teaspoon salt
1/2 teaspoon dry
   mustard
1/2 cup vegetable oil
1/2 onion, finely
   chopped
1 tablespoon fresh
   papaya seeds

1 Put vinegar and dry ingredients in a blender. With motor running, add oil in a steady stream, then add onion. Add papaya seeds and blend only until seeds resemble coarsely ground pepper. Chill one hour before serving. Makes one cup.

VINAIGRETTE SALAD DRESSING

1 Mash garlic and salt between layers of a brown paper bag until almost a paste. Put into food processor. Add pepper, mustards, cream and olive oil. Turn machine on. Slowly add vinegar and lemon juice, then add vegetable oil drop by drop until thoroughly mixed.

1 garlic clove, peeled
1/2 teaspoon coarse salt
1/2 teaspoon freshly
ground pepper
1/2 teaspoon dry
mustard
1 teaspoon Dijon
mustard
2 tablespoons whipping
cream
2 tablespoons olive oil
2 tablespoons wine
vinegar
1 teaspoon fresh lemon
juice
1/4 cup vegetable oil

WAIMEA MEADOW

By Kathy Long

Born in Texas, educated in Finland, long time Waimea resident, Kathy Long has become one of the best known and most successful artists on the Island. Because of her skill and penchant for realism, Kathy has been subject to many compliments, perhaps the greatest being that many people commission her to paint their most precious and prized family members. Kathy lives in Waimea with her husband and two children.

MEATS

MARTY'S FLANK STEAK

KIWI VEAL

TRISHA'S MEATBALLS

APRICOT PORK CHOPS

PORK CHOPS SADAKO

PORK CHOPS WITH
RASPBERRY VINEGAR SAUCE

SPARERIBS WITH PICKLED VEGETABLES

POT TUA

ROAST LAMB SHANKS

MARTY'S FLANK STEAK

1 cup salad oil
3/4 cup soy sauce
1/4 cup Worcestershire
  sauce
2 tablespoons dry
  mustard
2-1/4 teaspoons garlic
  salt
1 tablespoon coarsely
  ground pepper
1/2 cup dry sherry
3 tablespoons fresh
  parsley, chopped
1/3 cup fresh lemon
  juice

1 Combine all ingredients. Let flank steaks marinate six to twelve hours (can sit overnight). Preheat grill and cook flank steaks.

2 Serve sliced on the diagonal across the grain.

Note: *It's a great idea to cook extra steaks and use your leftovers for fajitas.*

KIWI VEAL

4 fresh kiwis, peeled
1/3 cup kiwi preserves
1/4 cup crystallized
  ginger
2 tablespoons dry white
  wine
1-1/2 pounds veal,
  pounded into 18
  medallions
Flour, all purpose
2 tablespoons olive oil
Fresh kiwi slices

1 In food processor, purée four kiwis, preserves, ginger and white wine until smooth. In a small saucepan, heat mixture over low heat while preparing veal. Lightly dust veal medallions in flour. Sauté veal in hot oil about two minutes per side. Pour heated kiwi sauce onto four plates. Top with veal. Garnish with kiwi slices.

TRISHA'S MEATBALLS

1 Mix together and form into small balls. Place in a greased flat baking dish. Cover with barbecue sauce. Place tin foil over pan and bake at 350 degrees for 45 minutes. Remove foil for last 10 minutes, if desired, to thicken sauce.

1-1/2 pounds lean ground beef
1/2 to 3/4 cup oatmeal (or 1 cup bread crumbs)
Dash of milk
1 egg
Salt
Pepper
1 small onion, chopped
Garlic powder

BARBECUE SAUCE

1 Mix and simmer for 30 minutes, uncovered, stirring occasionally.

1/3 to 1/2 cup vinegar
1 clove garlic, minced
1/4 cup butter, or less
1/2 teaspoon pepper
1/2 teaspoon paprika, optional
1 teaspoon salt
2 teaspoons molasses
2 tablespoons water
2 teaspoons Worcestershire sauce
1 cup catsup
2 tablespoons soy sauce

APRICOT PORK CHOPS

6 pork chops, 1/2"-1"
  thick
1-16 ounce can apricot
  halves, drained
Barbecue sauce

1 For each serving, place pork chops on square of heavy aluminum foil; top with two to three (or more if desired) apricot halves. Top meat and apricots with two tablespoons (or more) barbecue sauce. Close foil over meat, double folding edges on top and sides. Bake at 400 degrees for 35 minutes.

Serves 6.

Note: *Two pork chops can be cooked in one foil wrap. Make sure to have something oven-proof and flat underneath to support weight.*

PORK CHOPS SADAKO

8 pork chops
Salt
Pepper
Garlic powder
2-4 round onions,
  sliced
4 tablespoons soy sauce
4 tablespoons dark
  brown sugar
3 tablespoons cider
  vinegar
3 teaspoons fresh
  ginger, grated

1 Season the chops with salt, pepper and garlic powder, then brown in hot pan. Place browned chops in a casserole dish and cover with sliced onions. Combine the soy sauce, sugar, vinegar, and grated ginger into a sauce and pour over the chops and onions. Cover and bake at 350 degrees for an hour.

PORK CHOPS WITH RASPBERRY VINEGAR SAUCE

1 Dredge chops in flour, shake off excess. Season both sides with salt, pepper and rosemary. Sauté garlic in oil for one minute. Add pork chops and brown. Pour off fat from the pan. Stir in beef stock and vermouth. Cover and simmer 20 to 30 minutes. Remove chops from pan and keep warm.

2 Turn heat to high. Reduce sauce in pan until thick. Add the vinegar and continue cooking until thickened. Add cream and simmer until sauce is thick enough to coat chops. Taste and adjust seasoning.

3 Arrange chops on platter. Spoon sauce over chops.

4 Serve immediately.

Serves 4.

4 boneless pork chops
2 tablespoons flour
Salt
1/4 teaspoon white
  pepper
1/2 teaspoon dried
  rosemary
1 clove garlic, pressed
2 tablespoons oil
1/2 cup beef stock
1/2 cup dry vermouth
1/4 cup raspberry
  vinegar
1/4 cup heavy cream

SPARERIBS WITH PICKLED VEGETABLES

1 pound spareribs,
  Chinese style
2 tablespoons vinegar
1/2 cup water
3 tablespoons brown
  sugar
1-1/8 tablespoons
  cornstarch

1 Brown spareribs in oil. Remove excess oil.

2 Mix vinegar, water and sugar. Let stand for 15 minutes and add to spareribs. Simmer slowly until tender. Remove spareribs to heated plate and keep warm. Add cornstarch to sauce and stir to thicken. Add spareribs to sauce and serve over pickled vegetables.

PICKLED VEGETABLES

1 pound each turnips,
  carrots and cucumbers,
  sliced
2 tablespoons vinegar
3 tablespoons brown
  sugar
1 teaspoon salt
2 tablespoons ginger,
  sliced fine

1 Mix vinegar, brown sugar, salt and ginger. Pour over sliced vegetables and marinate overnight.

POT TUA (PORK WITH CASHEWS)

1 Coat pork with soy sauce and marinate a few hours. Heat oil and brown garlic. Add pork and stir fry until brown. Add brown sugar and cook until melted. Add and toss cashews. Heat through. Serve over rice.

Serves 4.

1 to 1-1/2 pounds pork, cut into bite size pieces
3-4 tablespoons soy sauce
5 tablespoons oil
6-7 cloves garlic, chopped
1/2 cup brown sugar
1/4 pound cashews, roasted

ROAST LAMB SHANKS

1 Put shanks in kettle with celery tops, parsley, bay leaf, thyme, rosemary and garlic. Add enough boiling water to barely cover the meat. Cook slowly for one hour, adding salt and pepper toward the end of cooking time.

2 Remove the shanks and place them in a shallow baking pan. Save the pan juices. Roast shanks in a 375 degree oven for 1 hour or until crisply browned, turning occasionally and basting frequently with the wine mixed with the oil. When done, make gravy in same pan, using the strained broth in which the shanks were cooked.

Note: *Extra broth makes great soup stock*

4 meaty lamb shanks
1 bunch celery tops
1 bay leaf
Sprig of parsley
Pinch of thyme
Pinch of rosemary
1 clove garlic
1 1/2 teaspoons salt
1/4 teaspooon pepper
1/2 cup flour
1/2 cup salad oil
1 cup claret wine

PARKER RANCH HOUSE

By Jane Thronas

Jane Thronas was raised in Waimea on the Big Island. She graduated from the
Hawaii Preparatory Academy, where her father was headmaster from 1954 to 1975,
and the University of Hawaii at Manoa. She now teaches art to grades K through
8 at H.P.A. Her watercolors and mixed media reflect a life long love for the islands.

POULTRY

CHICKEN BREASTS WITH MAC NUT PESTO
CHICKEN STROGANOFF
CHINESE POT ROAST CHICKEN
CURRIED CHICKEN & SHRIMP
MANGO CHICKEN
MARINATED BARBEQUED TURKEY
MICROWAVE KALUA TURKEY

CHICKEN BREASTS WITH MAC NUT PESTO

Pesto Sauce:
2 cups fresh basil leaves
3 cloves garlic
1/4 cup macadamia
 nuts
1/2 teaspoon salt
1/2 cup olive oil
1/2 cup parmesan
 cheese, grated

Filling:
1/4 cup macadamia
 nuts
1 pound fresh spinach
2 tablespoons butter
1 medium onion,
 chopped
1/2 cup ricotta cheese
1/4 cup pesto sauce
1 egg yolk
1/8 teaspoon black
 pepper
Salt to taste

4 slices prosciutto,
 halved
4 large whole chicken
 breasts, skinned,
 boned, halved, and
 flattened
3 tablespoons butter
3 tablespoons fresh
 lemon juice

1 TO PREPARE PESTO SAUCE: In food processor with steel blade, process basil and garlic, add nuts and salt. With machine running, pour olive oil in thin stream through feed tube; process until blended. Chill. (Can be frozen at this point). Before using, blend in Parmesan. Makes one cup.

2 TO PREPARE FILLING: Preheat oven to 350 degrees. Toast nuts in oven for three minutes; set aside. In ten inch skillet, steam spinach over medium heat for two minutes. Remove from heat; drain. Rinse in cold water to stop cooking process. Place spinach in dry towel and squeeze until all excess liquid is gone. Chop medium-fine. In small skillet, sauté onion in butter over low heat; set aside. In a large bowl, combine nuts, spinach, onions, cheese, pesto, yolk, pepper and salt.

3 TO ASSEMBLE: Preheat oven to 375 degrees. Place half slice prosciutto on each chicken breast. Spread filling evenly over prosciutto. Beginning with small end, roll up chicken. Place chicken rolls seam down in a greased medium baking dish. Melt butter, remove from stove and add lemon juice; spoon over chicken. Bake 25 to 30 minutes, basting with pan juices. Chill. Slice chicken. Lighten remaining pesto with 4 tablespoons mayonnaise and serve with chicken.

Serves 6 - 8.

CHICKEN STROGANOFF

1 Dredge chicken in seasoned flour. Sauté in oil and 2 tablespoons of butter until golden, about 5 minutes. Remove from pan and set aside. Cook shallots in saucepan with two tablespoons butter until softened. Add mushrooms and sage and cook, stirring, until mushrooms give off their juices.

2 Add brandy and simmer until liquid is almost evaporated. Add chicken broth, bring to a boil. Reduce heat and simmer for 3 minutes. Stir in chicken and heat until sauce is slightly thickened. Stir in parsley, mustard, Worcestershire sauce and sour cream. Cook over low heat, stirring, until hot, don't let boil. Serve with noodles or rice.

Serves 4.

2 whole chicken breasts, boneless, skinless, cut into 1" pieces

Seasoned flour:
1/4 cup flour
Salt and pepper

2 tablespoons olive oil
1/4 cup unsalted butter
1/2 cup shallots, minced
1/2 pound mushrooms, sliced
1/2 teaspoon dry sage, crumbled
2 tablespoons brandy
1 cup chicken broth
3 tablespoons fresh parsley, minced
1 teaspoon Dijon mustard
1 teaspoon Worcestershire sauce
1/2 cup sour cream

CHINESE POT ROAST CHICKEN

3 pounds chicken
  thighs, skinless
1/2 teaspoon salt
1/4 cup soy sauce
3 tablespoons olive oil
6 dried mushrooms,
  soaked, washed and
  quartered
1 small piece of ginger
  root, minced (or 1/4
  teaspoon powdered)
1 cup Chinese peas
  (snow peas)
2 green onions, cut in
  1" slices
1 tablespoon cornstarch
1 cup chicken stock
1 tablespoon soy sauce
1 teaspoon sugar

1 Rub chicken with salt and marinate in 1/4 cup soy sauce for 15 minutes. Remove chicken from marinade and brown in oil. Add mushrooms, ginger, and one tablespoon water. Cover and simmer slowly for 30-45 minutes. Place chicken on serving dish and keep warm (leave mushrooms in skillet). Add peas and onions. Combine remaining ingredients and add to mushroom mixture. Cook until sauce thickens. Pour over chicken and serve.

Serves 4 to 6.

CURRIED CHICKEN & SHRIMP

1 Cut chicken into 1-1/2" strips. Shell and devein shrimp; rinse and drain. Heat 1 tablespoon of butter in small saucepan. Add onion and garlic. Cook briefly and add celery. Cook, stirring for 1 minute. Sprinkle with curry powder and stir. Add tomato, banana, apple and bay leaf. Add broth, salt and pepper. Stir well. Simmer 10 minutes. Heat remaining butter in skillet and add chicken. Stir and cook 3 minutes. Add shrimp and cook, stirring, about 2 minutes. Remove from heat, set aside. Remove bay leaf from sauce and pour into blender (or food processor). Blend to fine texture. Pour sauce over chicken mixture. Bring to simmer for 2 minutes. Stir and serve.

2 chicken breasts, boneless, skinless
1 pound medium size shrimp
2 tablespoons butter
1/2 cup onion, chopped
1 teaspoon garlic, chopped
1/2 cup celery, chopped
2 tablespoons curry powder
2 small tomatoes, cut into small cubes
1 small banana, cut into 1/2" cubes
1 cup apples, peeled and cubed
1 bay leaf
2 cups chicken broth
Salt and pepper

MANGO CHICKEN

4 boneless chicken
   breast halves
1 tablespoon dry sherry
3 tablespoons soy sauce
2 teaspoons sesame oil
4 teaspoons cornstarch
1 ginger root, one inch,
   peeled and minced
4 cloves garlic, crushed
4 green onions, white
   parts with bits of
   green, thinly sliced
1 red bell pepper, seeded
   and sliced thinly
1/2 cup chicken broth
2 tablespoons peanut oil
1 tablespoon fresh lime
   juice
1 teaspoon sugar
2 large fresh mangoes,
   peeled and sliced

1 Cut chicken into 3 inch wide strips. Place in bowl with sherry, 1 tablespoon soy sauce 1 teaspoon sesame oil, 2 teaspoons cornstarch and half of the minced ginger. Combine remaining 2 teaspoons of cornstarch with chicken broth, stirring to dissolve.

2 Heat peanut oil in non-stick wok or skillet over high heat. Add garlic, red pepper and ginger and stir fry 1 minute. Add chicken and stir fry 5 minutes or until no longer pink. Add remaining 1 to 2 tablespoons of soy sauce and green onions and cook for a few seconds. Stir in chicken broth-cornstarch mixture and heat until bubbly. Add lime juice, mango slices, sugar and remaining sesame oil. Cook for a few seconds just to heat through. Serve with white rice.

Note: *This recipe can be made with pheasant or similar game as well.*

MARINATED BARBECUED TURKEY

1 Cut up turkey into sections, put aside.

2 In large pan add grapefruit juice, lemon juice, soy sauce, sesame oil and olive oil. Add to this mixture brown sugar, mashed garlic cloves and onion. Stir to blend. Add all fresh herbs and pepper. Taste to see if mixture is sweet enough, if not add more brown sugar. Marinate for 5 hours, turning turkey over at least once. Remove turkey from mixture and cook on grill. You may use marinade to baste.

*1 whole turkey or turkey
 sections
3 cups grapefruit juice,
 freshly squeezed
1/2 cup lemon juice,
 freshly squeezed
9 cloves garlic, mashed
1 sweet onion, chopped
 finely
2/3 cup soy sauce or
 teriyaki sauce
2 tablespoons sesame oil
1 cup olive oil
1/4 cup brown sugar
1/2 cup fresh tarragon
1/4 cup fresh parsley
1/4 cup fresh sage
1/2 teaspoon pepper*

MICROWAVE KALUA TURKEY

1 Thaw turkey and tie legs, soften butter in pyrex container, add rest of ingredients. Rub over turkey. Place breast down in cooking bag. Tie with string. Puncture near tie. Place on deep microwaveable dish. Be sure bag doesn't hang over dish. Microwave on high for 5 minutes per pound.

2 Turn turkey over. Poke with 6 more holes on top of bag. Microwave at 70% for 4 minutes per pound. Let stand 15 minutes. Remove turkey, shred. Pour liquid over until desired taste.

*12-14 pound turkey
1/2 cup butter, softened
2 tablespoons Hawaiian
 salt (coarse salt)
2 tablespoons liquid
 smoke
2 tablespoons kitchen
 bouquet
1 cooking bag*

BUSTER BROWN

By Marcia Ray

Originally from Florida, Marcia Ray has lived in Hawaii since 1973. She studied art at the University of Arizona and at the Art Academy in Ridgewood, New Jersey. Marcia draws and paints Hawaii from deep underwater "fantaseas" to cloudscapes and all the in-between. She considers our Big Island to be "a Kaleidoscope of colors always blessing us with an incredible show."

SEAFOOD

CREAMED BAKED FISH

TRES HOMBRES' FISH TACOS

MAHI MAHI MEXICANA

ZESTY GRILLED FISH

ONO ONO BAKED FISH

PEPPERED HAWAIIAN FISH WITH ASIAN SLAW

SIMPLE BLACKENED FISH

TUNA WITH TARRAGON MUSTARD SAUCE

HERB GARLIC SHRIMP KABOBS

ONO SCAMPI

CREAMED BAKED FISH

6 pieces mahimahi,
  sliced 1/2" thick
1 egg, beaten
3/4 teaspoon
  Worcestershire sauce
1 cup cheddar cheese,
  grated

White Sauce:
4 tablespoons butter
4 tablespoons flour
2 cups milk

1 Butter an 9 x 11 casserole dish and sprinkle bottom with 1/4 cup grated cheese.

2 Dip fish into beaten egg then place in casserole dish. Prepare white sauce, adding Worcestershire sauce and pour over fish.

3 Sprinkle remaining cheese on top and bake at 350 degrees for 45 minutes.

TRES HOMBRES' FISH TACOS

1 Grill tortilla lightly to soften. Fill with fish, cabbage, tomato and sprinkle with cheese. Garnish with lime.

1 pound fish, batter
  fried (recipe below)
8 -10" flour tortillas
16 ounces white
  cabbage, shredded
1 cup tomatoes, diced
1 cup cheddar cheese,
  grated
1 cup tartar sauce
Lime wedges

JALAPENO BATTER

1 Using mixer, slowly combine flour and beer in large bowl. When smooth, add remaining ingredients and mix for 5 minutes. Can be refrigerated.

4 cups flour
60 ounces beer (let
  stand until flat)
3 jalapenos, diced
1/2 crushed red chili

MAHI MAHI MEXICANA

5-6 ounces fillet of
  mahimahi, skinless
2 tablespoons flour
1 large egg, beaten
2 tablespoons milk
1/4 cup cheddar cheese,
  shredded
1/4 cup Monterey Jack
  cheese, shredded
2 tablespoons Parmesan
  cheese
3 ounces green chile
  salsa

1 Debone fillet, lightly roll in flour, then dip in egg wash (combine egg and milk). Sauté until completely done or to your wishes. Place in small casserole dish suitable for oven or broiler use. Top liberally with salsa, then Jack, followed by cheddar cheese. Sprinkle the Parmesan cheese over the entire dish and place under the broiler or in the oven until Parmesan turns to a golden brown.

2 Garnish with lemons and parsley.

ZESTY GRILLED FISH

1 Arrange fish in single layer. Combine marinade ingredients and pour over fish. Let stand at room temperature 30 minutes to one hour. Preheat barbecue grill. Grill fish approximately 4 minutes on each side until fish flakes.

Ono, ahi or marlin steaks, 1" thick

Marinade:
6 tablespoons soy sauce
6 tablespoons orange juice
3 tablespoons olive oil
3 tablespoons catsup
3 tablespoons fresh parsley, chopped
2 cloves garlic, chopped
1-1/2 teaspoons fresh lemon juice
3/4 teaspoon dried oregano, crumbled
3/4 teaspoon freshly ground pepper

ONO ONO BAKED FISH

Fish, any type, filleted
Ti leaves (aluminum
  foil may be substituted)
Mayonnaise
Lemon, sliced thin
Onion, sliced into large
  rings
Mushrooms, 3-4 per
  fillet, sliced
Butter or margarine
Garlic powder
Parsley, salt, pepper

1 In a shallow baking pan, place several layers of ti leaves (or aluminum foil). Lay fish fillets on top. Spread both sides of fish with mayonnaise. Place one to two slices of lemon on each fillet, followed by one large onion ring. Place sliced mushroom inside of onion and top with one teaspoon of butter or margarine. Sprinkle with garlic powder, parsley, salt, and pepper to taste. Cover tightly with ti leaf or tin foil. Bake in 350 degree oven for 20-30 minutes per pound.

PEPPERED HAWAIIAN FISH WITH ASIAN SLAW

From Alan Wong of the Canoe House

1 Rub fish with 1 tablespoon peanut oil. Sprinkle with pepper. In the remaining oil, sauté the fish. Spoon some of the vinaigrette over the fish.

1-1/2 pounds ahi, cut into 12 equal portions
2 tablespoons peanut oil
Coarsely ground pepper

ASIAN SLAW & VINAIGRETTE

1 Mix all ingredients together with half of the vinaigrette.

1 cup pea pods, cut lengthwise into slivers
1 cup carrots, shredded
2 cups Waimea or regular cabbage, finely cut
2 medium size (2/3 pound) firm-ripe tomatoes, cut into wedges

VINAIGRETTE

1 Heat ginger and oil on medium high until golden brown, 2-3 minutes. Remove from heat and stir in remaining ingredients.

2 TO SERVE: Arrange equal portions of slaw and tomatoes on 4 plates. Place fish on plate, spoon remaining vinaigrette over fish and tomatoes.

Serves 4.

1/2 cup fresh ginger, cut finely into slivers
1-1/2 tablespoons Oriental sesame oil
1/4 cup soy sauce
1-1/2 tablespoons rice vinegar
1-1/2 tablespoons Mirin
1-1/2 tablespoons sugar
1-1/2 tablespoons lime juice
1 small clove garlic, minced

SIMPLE BLACKENED FISH

Ahi fish fillets, 1/2"
  thick
Equal amounts of:
Curry powder
Chile powder
Paprika
Garlic salt
Olive oil
Butter or margarine

A delicious, fail-proof, simple "blackened" dish that tastes just right every time and does not burn the pan or fill the house with smoke!

1 Mix equal parts of four spices. Dredge moist fillets in spice mixture and sauté in hot butter and olive oil for 3 minutes on each side.

Note: *Skinless, boneless chicken breasts or thighs may be substituted. Cover pan and be sure to cook chicken all the way through.*

TUNA STEAKS WITH TARRAGON MUSTARD SAUCE

1 Chop 4 tablespoons macadamia nuts and mix with bread crumbs, salt and pepper. Dredge tuna steaks in crumbs. Mix beaten egg and water. Dip tuna steaks into egg wash and dredge in crumbs again. Set aside. In large skillet, heat oil. Fry tuna steaks for 10 minutes per inch of thickness. Do not crowd. Drain on paper towels and place on warm platter. Serve with mustard sauce and garnish with toasted nuts.

4 tuna steaks, 6-8
  ounces each
1 egg, beaten
1/2 cup water
3/4 cup vegetable oil
4 tablespoons
  macadamia nuts
1 cup dry bread crumbs
Whole macadamia
  nuts, toasted
Salt and pepper

TARRAGON MUSTARD SAUCE

1 In medium saucepan, melt butter. Add wine, tarragon and mustard. Simmer until reduced by third or by half. Stirring constantly, pour in cream. Simmer 1 minute. Season with salt and pepper and serve over tuna.

3 tablespoons unsalted
  butter
1/2 cup dry white wine
1 teaspoon dried
  tarragon
2 teaspoons Dijon
  mustard
1/4 cup heavy cream
Salt and pepper to taste

HERB & GARLIC SHRIMP KABOBS

1 pound shrimp, 21-26
  count, peeled
3/4 teaspoon salt
1/2 teaspoon oregano
1/2 teaspoon thyme
  leaves
4 tablespoons butter
4 tablespoons oil
4 cloves garlic, finely
  minced
1 tablespoon minced
  parsley
12 whole, fresh
  mushrooms
12 cherry tomatoes

1 Toss shrimp with salt, oregano, and thyme. Chill for about 30 minutes.

2 Melt butter and oil, add the minced garlic and parsley, set aside.

3 Thread 3 shrimps on each skewer, spacing with a cherry tomato and a mushroom. Place in baking pan and brush each kabob with the garlic butter.

4 Bake in a preheated 375 degree oven for 12 to 15 minutes, being careful not to overcook.

5 Serve on a bed of pilaf or wild rice.

Makes 4 servings of 2 skewers each.

ONO SCAMPI

1 Sauté the onion and garlic in the butter. Add the salt, pepper, lemon thyme, and oregano. When the onions begin to soften, add the ono. Cover for 5 minutes. Stir until fish is nearly done and add the tomato. When the tomato softens, add the flour slowly to the dish and stir until the sauce thickens. Sprinkle the parsley over the top and serve.

1 medium onion, diced
1-1/2 cloves garlic,
  chopped fine
1/2 cup butter
Dash of salt and pepper
1 teaspoon oregano,
  more to taste
Dash of lemon thyme
1 medium tomato,
  diced
3 pounds ono, diced
  bite size
1 tablespoon flour
1 tablespoon fresh
  parsley, chopped fine

COWBIRDS

By Candace Peterson

A native of northern California and a graduate of Diablo Valley College, Candace Peterson's greatest teacher has been nature and its creatures. Challenged and encouraged by her love for the outdoors, Peterson's watercolors feature a combination of reality, fantasy and color. She captures the meaning, as well as the beauty, of Hawaii's landscapes in her paintings. Candace lives in Waimea with her husband and three of their youngest children.

SOUPS, STEWS & CASSEROLES

HAWAIIAN PUMPKIN SOUP

MEXICAN CHICKEN RICE SOUP

WAIMEA SOUP

TURKEY BARLEY SOUP

GREEN CHILE CORN BAKE

GRATIN OF LENTILS & CARROTS

MIXED BEANS CHRISTINE

LOW FAT TURKEY ENCHILADAS

WILD RICE & SAUSAGE CASSEROLE

CHEESY SPINACH MAIN DISH

SPAGHETTI PIE

HAWAIIAN PUMPKIN SOUP

1 garlic head, unpeeled
2 pounds pumpkin,
    unpeeled, cut into 8
    pieces, seeds removed
1 large onion,
    unpeeled, cut
    vertically in half
2 tablespoons olive oil
8 fresh thyme sprigs, or
    2 teaspoons dried,
    crumbled
1/2 cup whipping
    cream
1-3/4 cups or more
    chicken stock

1 Preheat oven to 350 degrees. Cut 1/3 inch off top of garlic head. Arrange garlic, pumpkin and onion cut side up in large baking dish. Drizzle vegetables with oil and sprinkle with thyme. Cover dish tightly with foil and bake until pumpkin is tender when pierced with knife, about 1 1/2 hours. Uncover vegetables and cool 15 minutes.

2 Scrape pumpkin from skin into processor bowl. Peel outer layers and trim root end from onion halves, add onion to processor. Separate 9 garlic cloves from head; peel and add to processor. Add any juices from baking pan. Add cream and purée until almost smooth. Taste, adding more garlic if stronger flavor is desired.

3 Transfer purée to large, heavy sauce pan. Whisk in 1-3/4 cups chicken stock. Stir over medium heat until heated through, adding more broth if thinner consistency is desired. Season with salt and pepper.

Can be prepared one day ahead.

MEXICAN CHICKEN RICE SOUP

1 Drain tomatoes, reserving liquid, and chop; set aside. Sauté onion, celery and garlic in oil about two minutes. Stir in rice, cumin, and pepper. Add chicken broth, tomato and tomato liquid. Bring to boil. Cover and simmer 15 minutes. Add diced chicken and corn, simmer about 2 minutes. Remove from heat. Stir in lime juice and fresh cilantro. Serve hot.

Serves 8.

1-15 ounce can tomatoes
1 cup green onion, sliced
1 cup celery, sliced
1 tablespoon garlic, finely chopped
1 tablespoon vegetable oil
1 cup rice
1-1/2 teaspoons cumin
1/2 teaspoon pepper
9 cups chicken broth
1 whole chicken breast, skinned, boned and diced
1-10 ounce package frozen corn, thawed
2 tablespoons lime juice
2 tablespoons cilantro, chopped

WAIMEA SOUP

Soup:
2 tablespoons butter
1 tablespoon olive oil
4 cups sweet onions, thinly
*   sliced*
3 tablespoons flour
1-16 ounce can tomato
*   puree*
7 cups beef broth
2 cloves garlic, crushed
1 tablespoon red wine
*   vinegar*
1 tablespoon Worcestershire
*   sauce*
1 tablespoon sugar
1-1/2 teaspoons salt
1/4 teaspoon each oregano,
*   tarragon, ground pepper,*
*   chili pepper water or*
*   Tabasco*
1/2 teaspoon cumin

Condiments:
2 Linguesa, cooked, sliced
1 pound chicken, cooked,
*   shredded*
1 cup red and/or yellow
*   bell peppers, diced*
1 cup cucumbers, peeled,
*   diced*
1 cup red tomato, diced
1 cup green onion,
*   chopped fine*

1/2 pound carrots, diced
3 eggs, hard
*   boiled,chopped*
1 cup sour cream
1 cup cheddar, grated
1-8 ounce can garbanzo
*   beans*
1-2 ounce can sliced
*   black olives*
1-1/2 cups rice, cooked

Delicious and crunchy; this soup is best made with the freshest garden vegetables you can find.

1 Sauté onions over low heat in butter and olive oil until transparent, about 45 minutes. Mix flour in well then slowly add tomato purée and beef broth. Add remaining basic soup ingredients and bring to a boil; turn to low and let simmer 30 minutes.   All condiments are served separately. Serve the soup piping hot, and let your guests add the condiments of their choice.

Serves 6.

TURKEY BARLEY SOUP

Great winter soup!

1 Break up carcass and bones as much as possible and put them in a large soup kettle. Add all ingredients, except barley. Cover and simmer gently for 1 hour, then add barley and continue to simmer for another hour. Strain and remove bones. Serve with garlic bread and green salad.

1 turkey carcass, not totally picked over
1 onion, coarsely chopped
3 carrots
1 cup dry white wine
1 bunch celery, coarsely chopped
1 teaspoon thyme
1 teaspoon basil
1 teaspoon chervil
1 can vegetable juice
Salt, pepper
1 cup barley
Water

GREEN CHILE CORN BAKE

1 Mix creamed corn, corn meal, eggs, oil and garlic salt. Spread half of mixture in a greased 2 1/2 quart shallow baking dish. Scatter chopped chiles and half of the shredded cheese over the corn mixture. Spread remaining corn mixture, then top with remaining cheese. Bake at 375 degrees for 30-45 minutes until center is just set. Do not overcook.

Serves 6-8.

4 cups creamed corn
3/4 cup yellow corn meal
2 eggs, beaten
6 tablespoons oil
1 teaspoon garlic salt
2 cups cheddar cheese, shredded
2-3 ounce cans chopped green chiles

GRATIN OF LENTILS & CARROTS

1/4 cup olive oil
1 onion, finely chopped
6 carrots, thinly sliced
1 bay leaf
1 teaspoon dried thyme
3-1/2 cups chicken stock
2 cups dried lentils
1/2 cup parsley, finely
  chopped
2 tablespoons Dijon
  mustard
Salt and pepper

1 Heat 1/4 cup oil over medium heat and cook onion until translucent, about 5 minutes. Add carrots, bay leaf and thyme. Reduce heat to low. Cover and cook until carrots are just starting to soften, stirring occasionally, about 10 minutes. Add stock and bring to boil. Add lentils. Reduce heat. Cover and cook until lentils are tender and most of the stock is absorbed, occasionally stirring, about 30 minutes. Season with salt.

2 Transfer lentils to bowl and cool. Stir in parsley, mustard, and pepper.

3 Preheat oven to 400 degrees. Bake lentils about 15-20 minutes. Serve hot.

Serves 6 to 8.

MIXED BEANS CHRISTINE

1 Sauté sausage, drain well. Add onion and sauté a few more minutes. Add remaining ingredients. Simmer 30 minutes.

1 Portuguese sausage, quartered and cut in 1/4" lengths
1 large sweet onion, chopped
2 ears fresh corn, cut kernels off husk
1 large tomato, chopped
1 cup kidney beans
1 can chili with beans
2 cups catsup
1 cup lima beans
1 can black olives
2/3 cup sherry
1 cup sharp cheddar cheese, grated

LOW FAT TURKEY ENCHILADAS WITH GREEN TOMATILLOS

Green Tomatillo Sauce:
6 cups chicken broth or
  turkey stock
24 tomatillos, skinned,
  seeded and chopped
2 large green peppers,
  seeded and chopped
4 Anaheim peppers,
  seeded and chopped
5 medium sweet onions,
  chopped
1/4 cup cilantro, chopped
1/4 cup parsley, chopped
3 tablespoons ground
  cumin
1 tablespoon white pepper
1 tablespoon paprika
24 corn tortillas

Turkey Mixture:
2-1/2 pounds chopped
  cooked turkey
15 ounces ricotta low fat
  cheese
8 ounces cottage cheese -
  2% fat
6 ounces golden raisins
16 ounces low fat
  Monterey Jack cheese,
  grated
1 cup chicken or turkey
  stock
1 tablespoon white pepper
1 tablespoon cayenne
  pepper

1 Bring 6 cups of chicken broth or turkey stock to a boil for 3-5 minutes. Let simmer for 30 minutes. Add tomatillos, peppers, onions, cilantro and parsley to broth. Add the cumin, white pepper and paprika. Stir and simmer.

2 Combine cooked turkey with ricotta cheese, cottage cheese, 8 ounces of Jack cheese and raisins. If too dry, add more stock to moisten.

3 ASSEMBLING THE ENCHILADAS: Place 1 cup of tomatillo sauce on the bottom of a 9 x 11 baking dish. Dip heated tortilla on one side in remaining green sauce mixture. Place 4 tablespoons of the turkey mixture on the corn tortilla and roll. Place rolled tortilla in prepared baking dish. When all tortillas are rolled and in pan, cover with tomatillo sauce and sprinkle remaining grated cheese on top. Bake in 350 degree oven for 15 minutes, or until the cheese melts and begins to bubble. Serve hot.

WILD RICE & SAUSAGE CASSEROLE

1 Wash rice. Gradually pour rice into 3 cups boiling water. Reduce heat, cover and simmer, stirring occasionally until rice is tender and all water absorbed, about 30-40 minutes. (Or cook in rice cooker using 2-1/4 cup water). Set aside.

2 Melt butter in large skillet over medium high heat. Add onion and mushrooms and sauté until golden. Add sausage and cook until brown, about 3 minutes. Transfer to casserole. Add rice, parsley, sage, salt and pepper. Bake covered 20 minutes at 350 degrees. Serves 8.

3 FOR SAUSAGE: Mix all together in food processor. Refrigerate or freeze extra for other recipes. Delicious on pizza!

3/4 cup wild rice
1 teaspoon salt
1 cup onion, chopped
1/2 cup butter
1 cup mushrooms,
 chopped
1/2 cup sausage (below)
2 tablespoons fresh
 parsley, minced
1/2 teaspoon dried sage,
 crumbled
Salt and pepper, ground

Sausage:
1/2 pound lean ground
 pork
1/2 teaspoon salt
1 clove garlic, chopped
1/2 teaspoon pepper
1/2 teaspoon thyme
1/4 teaspoon fennel
1/8 teaspoon nutmeg
1/8 teaspoon suga
1/2 teaspoon basil
1/4 cup parsley, chopped

CHEESY SPINACH MAIN DISH

*1 pound very lean
  ground meat*
1 tablespoon salad oil
1 teaspoon salt
1 teaspoon pepper
*1 teaspoon garlic
  powder*
*1 yellow onion, finely
  chopped*
*1/2 pound fresh
  mushrooms, sliced*
*1-8 ounce can tomato
  sauce*
*1-8 ounce carton sour
  cream*
1/8 teaspoon basil
1/8 teaspoon oregano
8 ounces cottage cheese
*2-10 ounce packages
  frozen spinach,
  thawed, all liquid
  pressed out*
*1 cup Parmesan cheese,
  grated*
*1 cup Longhorn cheese,
  grated*

1 Brown meat in skillet and drain fat. Add onions, mushrooms, garlic powder, salt and pepper and simmer 5 minutes. In large bowl combine tomato sauce, sour cream, basil, and oregano. Stir in cottage cheese and add to meat mixture. Add spinach, 1/2 cup each of Parmesan and Longhorn cheese. Put mixture in greased casserole and cover with remaining cheeses. Bake uncovered at 350 degrees for 30 minutes.

1 To make crust, combine vermicelli with other "crust" ingredients. Chop mixture with a knife and press mixture into a 10-inch pie plate.

2 To make filling, cook ground beef, Italian sausage and onion together. Drain fat. Stir in remaining ingredients. Heat thoroughly.

3 To assemble pie, spread ricotta cheese on "crust." Top with filling and cover with mozzarella cheese. Bake at 350 degrees for 30 minutes or until golden brown.

6-8 servings.

1 cup ricotta cheese
6 ounces mozzarella
  cheese, shredded

Crust:
6 ounces thin spaghetti
  (vermicelli), cooked
  and drained
1 clove garlic, minced
1/4 cup butter
1/2 cup grated
  Parmesan cheese
1 large egg, beaten
1 tablespoon fresh basil

Filling:
1/2 pound ground beef
3/4 pound Italian
  sausage
1/2 cup chopped onion
1-15 ounce can tomato
  sauce
1-6 ounce can tomato
  paste
1 teaspoon sugar
1 tablespoon fresh basil
1 tablespoon fresh
  oregano
1/4 cup white wine

IMIOLA CHURCH

By Harry Wishard

Born in the plantation town of Pahala, Harry Wishard puts Hawaiian reality on canvas with a deft and experiential hand. Wishard is by profession, a house painting contractor. His hours away from work are spent hunting and fishing and enjoying time with Chelsea, his three year old daughter.

PASTA, RICE & POTATOES

CAPPELINI WITH SHRIMP & MUSHROOMS

MOROCCAN COUSCOUS

EGGPLANT & SPINACH RICE

ONO PASTA

WILLOW DRIVE POTATOES

PENNE WITH EGGPLANT & MOZZARELLA

SPAGHETTI MARINARA WITH CHICKEN

CAPPELINI WITH SHRIMP & MUSHROOMS

16 ounces angel hair
  pasta
Shrimp (or larger
  shrimp cut into small
  pieces)
8 ounces mushrooms,
  sliced
3 egg yolks
1 pint half and half
1/2 cup Romano cheese,
  grated
1/2 cup Parmesan
  cheese, grated
1/2 cup margarine,
  melted

1 Cook pasta; set aside. Over low heat, mix egg yolks, half and half, Romano and Parmesan cheeses in a small sauce pan to make sauce. Sauté sliced mushrooms and shrimp in margarine. Add sauce to mushroom and shrimp mixture. Pour over pasta and serve.

MOROCCAN COUSCOUS

2 tablespoons olive oil
1 large onion, finely
  sliced
2 zucchinis, cut into
  julienne
2 carrots, peeled and
  cut into julienne
2-1/4 cups chicken stock
  or canned broth
1 cup golden raisins
3/4 teaspoon ground
  cinnamon
1/4 teaspoon turmeric
1-1/2 cups couscous

1 Heat olive oil in heavy saucepan over medium heat. Add onion and sauté 5 minutes. Add zucchini and carrots, cook 5 minutes, stirring occasionally. Add chicken stock, golden raisins, cinnamon and turmeric. Season to taste with salt and pepper. Bring to boil. Mix in couscous. Cover, remove from heat and let stand 10 minutes.

EGGPLANT & SPINACH RICE

1 Scoop out pulp from eggplant halves (can use a grapefruit knife), leaving 1/4 inch thickness of pulp and peel. Score the pulp left in the eggplant shell. Cut up the pulp you have scooped out. Place diced pulp into a large skillet with olive oil, garlic, lemon juice and rice. Sauté for a few minutes, stirring well. Add liquid from canned tomatoes, salt and oregano. Cook for several minutes, stirring well. Remove from heat. Add spinach, parsley and cheese. Place eggplant halves in a baking dish and fill with the mixture. Cut tomatoes into wedges and tuck into ends and garnish tops. Bake in a 375 degree oven for 45 minutes.

Serves 2.

1 medium eggplant, sliced in half lengthwise
5 tablespoons olive oil
1 large clove garlic, minced
1/2 lemon
1 cup cooked brown rice (or brown rice/ kashi or wild rice mix)
1-15 ounce can whole stewed tomatoes
1/2 teaspoon salt
1 teaspoon oregano
1 cup spinach, finely chopped
1 cup fresh parsley, chopped
3/4 cup Parmesan cheese, grated

ONO PASTA

1 eggplant, cut in cubes
1/4 pound prosciutto,
  cut in small chunks
1 garlic clove, minced
2 tablespoons olive oil
1 tablespoon butter
1/4 cup brandy
28 ounce can Italian
  crushed tomatoes
1/2 cup beef broth
1 tablespoon fresh
  oregano, chopped
1 pound radiatore,
  farfalle or curly pasta
1/4 cup Parmesan,
  grated

1 Sprinkle eggplant with salt and let drain in colander for an hour. Rinse, drain and pat dry with paper towels. Sauté prosciutto, garlic and eggplant in butter and oil over moderate heat, stirring occasionally until eggplant begins to turn golden. Add the brandy and cook for 30 seconds. Add the tomatoes, broth and oregano. Simmer, stirring occasionally for 30 minutes. Cook the pasta in salted water and drain. Toss the pasta and sauce and sprinkle with Parmesan.

Serves 6 to 8.

WILLOW DRIVE POTATOES

1 Preheat oven to 375 degrees. Peel and slice white potatoes and keep in cold water; pat dry with dish towel before layering - this will prevent them from browning.

2 Coat bottom of 8 x 11 baking pan with butter and arrange a few fresh sprigs of thyme in the center of pan. When served, this dish will be inverted onto a serving dish, so arrange your first layer of potatoes carefully. Add the second layer of squash for color and then a layer of apples. Stop and pour half of the butter over the first 3 layers. Season with salt, pepper and thyme. Add a layer of sweet potatoes, squash and top with a final layer of white potatoes. Season and pour remaining butter over top. The white potatoes should be heaped on top. Place a pan on top of dish for first 15 minutes to help press potatoes down. Remove pan from top of dish and cook for one hour until golden brown. Remove from oven and pour off excess butter and invert onto a serving dish.

4 medium white potatoes, thinly sliced
2 tart, firm apples peeled and sliced
1 sweet potato, peeled and sliced
1 butternut squash, peeled and sliced
1 acorn squash, peeled and sliced
1 cup clarified butter
Fresh thyme
Salt
Pepper

PENNE WITH EGGPLANT & MOZZARELLA

3 large eggplant, sliced
 into 1/4 rounds
Salt
6 cloves garlic, finely
 minced
1/2 cup extra virgin olive
 oil
2 large cans whole
 tomatoes with their
 juice
Handful basil, finely
 chopped
Handful parsley, finely
 chopped
3 small red chili peppers,
 finely minced (or 3
 teaspoons hot chili
 flakes)
1 pound box imported
 penne noodles
2 whole fresh
 mozzarella, cut into
 small pieces (processed
 cheese will not work!)
Parmesan cheese

1 Sprinkle sliced eggplant with salt, put into a colander, weight down with a pot filled with water and allow eggplant to drain overnight. Either barbecue the eggplant or broil until browned. Cut into strips. Sauté garlic in oil until slightly browned; add eggplant and stir thoroughly. Add tomatoes, crushing in the pan, basil, parsley and chili peppers or flakes. Cook down over low heat, stirring occasionally until you have a nice thick sauce. Season to taste with salt and pepper and a teaspoon of sugar if too salty.

2 Cook penne according to directions on box, taking care not to overcook. When ready to serve, add mozzarella to sauce, mix thoroughly until cheese is melted. Pour sauce over penne and serve immediately with freshly grated Parmesan cheese.

SPAGHETTI MARINARA
WITH CHICKEN

1 Cook fettuccine. Cook chicken breasts and cut into bite size pieces.

2 In large skillet combine olive oil and garlic. Cook gently over low heat, stirring occasionally until garlic is deep golden brown, about 8 minutes. Increase heat to high and add tomatoes that have been broken up (squeeze with hands if needed) along with the juice. Boil over medium-high heat, stirring occasionally until most of the liquid has evaporated and sauce is thick, approximately 20-30 minutes. Add chicken pieces and dried tomatoes. Cook a little longer; season with salt and pepper. Pour sauce over noodles and sprinkle on capers.

1 pound fettuccine noodles
4 boneless, skinless chicken breasts
2 tablespoons olive oil
10 medium cloves garlic, diced
1-35 ounce can peeled Italian tomatoes
1-3 ounce package dried tomatoes, chopped
Fresh ground pepper
Salt
2 tablespoons capers

WAIMEA BARN

By Clem Lam

Clem Lam is an architect in Waimea. He was born in San Francisco and grew up on Oahu. He enjoys playing the guitar, traveling, surfing and painting. Clem and his wife, Janet, have been residents of Waimea since 1980. They have one son, Carl, who attends H.P.A.

VEGETABLES

ACORN SQUASH WITH APPLE
OR MUSHROOM CHEESE FILLINGS

ASPARAGUS WITH
HAZELNUT BUTTER SAUCE

BARBECUED EGGPLANT

BAKED TOFU IN HERB BUTTER SAUCE

BRAISED LEEKS

COMPANY CARROTS

LIZIKA'S CAULIFLOWER CAPER

EGGPLANT STIR-FRY WITH TOFU

SKILLET CABBAGE

SWEET & SOUR RED CABBAGE

VEGETABLE SOUFFLE

BAKED BANANAS KEAUKAHA

ACORN SQUASH WITH APPLE OR MUSHROOM CHEESE FILLING

2 large acorn squash

Apple Filling:
2 medium apples,
  chopped
1/2 cup sweet onion,
  chopped
3 tablespoons margarine
2 cups low fat cottage
  cheese
1 lemon, juiced
Dash of cinnamon
3/4 cup fat reduced
  cheddar cheese, grated
1/2 cup walnuts or
  raisins, chopped,
  optional

Mushroom Cheese
Filling:
1 tablespoon butter
1/2 pound mushrooms,
  chopped
1 cup sweet onions,
  chopped
1 clove garlic, crushed
1/2 teaspoon fresh basil,
  chopped
1/4 cup parsley, chopped
1 cup low fat cottage
  cheese
3/4 cup rice, cooked
2 tablespoons dry white
  wine
Dash of salt and pepper

1 TO PREPARE SQUASH: Split squash in half, place on oiled tray or on tin foil face down with skin on top. Bake for 45 minutes at 350 degrees or until inside is tender enough to eat. Set aside.

2 FOR APPLE FILLING: Sauté apples and onions in margarine until onions are clear. In a large bowl combine apple mixture with cottage cheese, lemon juice, cheddar cheese and cinnamon. Add walnuts or raisins if desired. Stuff the cavity of the acorn squash with the apple filling and bake covered at 350 degrees for 15 to 20 minutes.

3 FOR MUSHROOM CHEESE FILLING: Sauté mushrooms, onions and garlic with butter; add salt and pepper. Combine sautéd mixture with basil, parsley, cottage cheese, rice, and wine in a bowl. Stuff the cavity of the acorn squash with mushroom mixture. Bake in oven uncovered for 25 to 30 minutes at 350 degrees.

ASPARAGUS WITH HAZELNUT BUTTER SAUCE

1 Steam asparagus over salted water until crisp tender and drain well. Reserve and keep warm.

2 Melt the butter in small saucepan and when hot but not brown, add the chopped nuts. Cook and stir until nuts are light brown, about 1 minute. Add the vinegar, (there will be loud hissing) Stir at once and serve immediately over warm asparagus.

2 pounds asparagus, trimmed and peeled
1/2 cup butter
4 ounces hazelnuts, finely chopped
2 teaspoons tarragon wine vinegar

BARBECUED EGGPLANT

1 Split eggplant lengthwise and make diagonal crisscross slashes. Sprinkle with salt and let sit in a colander for 1/2 hour. Wipe off moisture and salt. Make a marinade with peanut and sesame oils, garlic, ginger, soy sauce and Chinese parsley. Let stand for a few hours. Grill on barbecue until eggplant is tender. Can be served hot or at room temperature.

5-7 eggplants, Japanese style
Salt
5-6 cloves garlic, crushed
1/4 cup Chinese parsley, finely chopped
2 tablespoons ginger, finely minced
3/4 cup peanut oil
1 tablespoon sesame oil
1/4 cup soy sauce

BAKED TOFU IN HERB BUTTER SAUCE

1 block tofu, cut into 4
  or 5 slices
1/2 cup butter (can
  reduce butter by half if
  desired)
3 tablespoons soy sauce
1 teaspoon garlic,
  minced
1/2 teaspoon basil
1 teaspoon oregano
1/4 teaspoon thyme
1/2 teaspoon rosemary
1/4 teaspoon tarragon
3 or 4 mushrooms,
  sliced
1/4 cup green onions,
  chopped

1 Place tofu in baking pan. In a small sauce pan, melt butter, add soy sauce and spices. Pour over tofu and bake at 375 degrees for 8 minutes. Remove and top with mushrooms and green onions. Baste until well coated. Return to oven and bake 5 minutes more.

BRAISED LEEKS

6 leeks, green tops
  removed
4 tablespoons butter
6 tablespoons good
  quality extra virgin
  olive oil
3 chicken bouillon
  cubes
Mace

1 Split leeks lengthwise and wash so no sand remains. Heat oil and butter. Brown until golden on both sides. Add bouillon cubes and water to cover. Sprinkle a couple of pinches of mace and simmer gently until liquid has evaporated.

COMPANY CARROTS

1 Cook carrots until tender; drain. Mix remaining ingredients in a sauce pan; add carrots and sauté 10 minutes. Stir while cooking so carrots get coated.

Note: *This recipe may be doubled, but don't increase the butter and sugar mixture because you'll have too much.*

2 cups carrots, cut round
3 tablespoons butter, melted
2 tablespoons sugar
1/2 teaspoon paprika
Juice of 1/2 lemon

LIZIKA'S CAULIFLOWER CAPER

1 Brown garlic in olive oil; remove garlic. Make a paste using capers, anchovy filets and parsley. Add sourdough crumbs to pan in which garlic was browned and briefly toss crumbs with oil. Add caper paste to pan and toss until well blended. Steam cauliflower. Sprinkle caper crumb mixture over cauliflower and serve hot.

3 large cloves garlic
1/2 cup good olive oil
1/4 cup capers
4 anchovy filets
Handful of fresh parsley
2 cups fresh sourdough bread crumbs
1 head cauliflower

EGGPLANT STIR-FRY WITH TERIYAKI TOFU

6-8 packaged large
  Shiitake mushrooms
1 pound firm tofu
8 Japanese eggplants,
  cut diagonally 1/2"
  thick pieces
4 cloves garlic, crushed
1/3 cup peanut or
  canola oil
3 red and/or yellow
  peppers, sliced
1/2 pound mushrooms,
  sliced
2/3 cup teriyaki sauce
Thai hot chile sauce
Chinese parsley

Teriyaki Sauce:
6 ounces ginger, cut
  into 2" pieces and
  smashed
10 cloves garlic,
  crushed
3 cups soy sauce
2 cups brown sugar
1/3 cup honey
1/2 cup cooking sherry
  or Marsala

1 Prepare Shiitake mushrooms by soaking in water until soft.

2 Marinate tofu slices, approximately 1/2" thick in 2/3 cup teriyaki sauce for 1 hour. Bake at 350 degrees for 1 hour, turning once, until all sauce is absorbed and tofu firm. Set aside.

3 Salt eggplant pieces and let drain in colander for 2 hours. Rinse off all salt and pat dry. Precook in microwave for 3 minutes on high.

4 Brown garlic in peanut or canola oil. Add peppers, cook until softened, then add eggplant and mushrooms. Sauté, adding a little teriyaki sauce, salt and Thai hot chile sauce to taste. Slice tofu into strips, add to vegetable with finely chopped Chinese parsley. Toss lightly and serve.

5 TERIYAKI SAUCE: Combine all ingredients and simmer for 20 minutes, let cool. Store sauce in jar and use as needed.

SKILLET CABBAGE

1 Add all ingredients to hot oil: Add water to cover and cook until tender.

4 cups cabbage,
  chopped
1 cup green pepper,
  chopped
2 cups celery, chopped
2 large onions, chopped
1/4 cup cooking oil
2 tablespoons sugar
Salt and pepper to taste
1/4 cup water or more

SWEET & SOUR RED CABBAGE

1 Heat oil in heavy large saucepan over medium-high heat. Add onion and apple and sauté until golden, about 7 minutes. Add cabbage, vinegar, sugar and celery seed and cook until cabbage is crisp-tender and liquid is reduced to glaze, about 10 minutes. Mix in bacon. Season with salt and pepper.

2 tablespoons vegetable
  oil
1/2 onion, sliced
1/2 apple, peeled, cored,
  chopped
4 cups red cabbage,
  thinly sliced
1/4 cup apple cider
  vinegar
4 tablespoons sugar
1/4 teaspoon celery seed
1/4 cup Canadian
  bacon, diced

VEGETABLE SOUFFLÉ

Cauliflower:
1 large head of
  cauliflower
1/4 cup butter, melted
1/2 cup mayonnaise
1/4 cup Parmesan
  cheese, grated
2 tablespoons fresh
  parsley, chopped
1 tablespoon lemon
  juice
1/4 teaspoon salt
2 egg whites

Broccoli or Zucchini:
2 large heads broccoli
  or zucchini
2 egg whites, room
  temperature
1/4 teaspoon salt
1/2 cup Swiss cheese,
  shredded (use cheddar
  for zucchini)
1/2 cup mayonnaise

1 FOR CAULIFLOWER SOUFFLÉ: Boil whole head of cauliflower in lightly salted water. Drain and rinse in cold water to prevent over cooking. Put whole head in small casserole or soufflé dish. Pour melted butter over cauliflower. Mix together mayonnaise, Parmesan, parsley, lemon juice and salt. Beat egg whites until stiff and add to above mixture. Spread over cauliflower and bake at 350 degrees until brown, approximately 20 minutes. Serve at once.

2 FOR BROCCOLI SOUFFLÉ: Cut broccoli into spears (or slice zucchini), steam until tender. Place in shallow, buttered, oven proof pan. Beat egg whites until stiff peaks form. Fold in cheese and mayonnaise and spread over vegetables.

3 Broil 6" from heat for 4-6 minutes or until golden brown.

BAKED BANANAS KEAUKAHA

Originally from Hilo, Hawaii, this recipe is excellent with chicken, turkey, and island fish

6 to 8 baking bananas
2 tablespoons melted
  butter
1/2 cup fresh orange
  juice
Wee sprinkling of salt

1 Place the skinned bananas, whole, in a shallow baking dish. Mix butter, orange juice and salt together; pour over bananas.

2 Bake, covered, in 375 degree oven for 30 minutes. Remove cover and bake another 30 minutes.

3 If baking bananas are not available, apple bananas may be used. Any other variety gets mushy. Bake apple bananas only 30 minutes.

ANNA'S POND

By Loretta Viecelli

Having an artist-mother for inspiration, Loretta Viecelli had been introduced to art at an early age. 'Lor,' as she is known to friends, grew up in Michigan and did some traveling before moving to Hawaii. She loves to dance, swim and garden. Her creative interests extend into photography and coconut palm weaving, but her first love is executing personalized charcoal portraits, and she enjoys oil painting.

SAUCES & CONDIMENTS

PUNA'S MANGO CHUTNEY

CRANBERRY SAUCE

JALAPENO JELLY

MANGO CHUTNEY

PADDY'S PICKLED PINEAPPLE

PAPAYA SALSA

SPICY CORN SALSA

KADIE'S FAMOUS MARINADE

TERIYAKI MARINADE

ORANGE BUTTER

LILIKOI BUTTER

PUNA'S MANGO CHUTNEY

6 quarts sliced mangoes

1 quart white vinegar

1-16 ounce package
  raisins

1 handful rock salt

2-1/2 quarts brown
  sugar

6 thumb size pieces
  ginger, peeled and
  chopped

1 medium onion,
  chopped

30 or more Hawaiian
  chili peppers, remove
  seeds

1 cup blanched
  almonds, chopped or
  sliced

1 whole head garlic,
  peeled and chopped

2 teaspoons cinnamon

1 teaspoon cloves

1 teaspoon nutmeg

1 teaspoon allspice

1 Peel and slice mangoes. Add vinegar, raisins, salt and sugar. Bring to boil while sugar melts.

2 Add ginger, onion, chili peppers, almonds, garlic, cinnamon, cloves, nutmeg and all spice to mangoes.

3 Boil 2 or more hours until fruit is glazed.

4 Put in sterile jars and seal.

CRANBERRY SAUCE

1 Crush or grind coarsely cranberries. Put into large heavy aluminum pot with 4 cups of water. Add sugar, rind of orange and diced lemon. Add 2 packages of Jell-O and stir.

2 Simmer at low heat for 4 hours until sauce is half of the total amount.

3 When sauce begins to thicken add macadamia nuts. Before removing from stove, add cream of tartar. Place in jars and refrigerate.

2 pounds fresh cranberries - crush or grind coarsely
4 cups water
2 cups sugar
Rind of 1 orange, cut in thin strips
1 teaspoon lemon rind, diced
2 packages of Jell-O (1 raspberry, 1 cherry)
1 can (small) macadamia nut bits (walnuts can be substituted)
2 teaspoons cream of tartar

JALAPENO JELLY

1 Clean, seed and chop peppers. Place in blender with vinegar. Blend well until chopped fine.

2 Place sugar in pot, add vinegar mixture and stir while bringing to a boil. Let stand for 10 minutes.

3 Add pectin and 2 drops color (red or green).

4 Pour into jelly jars. Cool at room temperature for 3 hours.

1 cup green bell pepper
6 - 8 jalapeno peppers (fresh or canned)
1-1/2 cups vinegar
3-1/2 cups sugar
6 ounces liquid pectin
4 -8 ounce jelly jars

MANGO CHUTNEY

5 pounds sliced mango
5 pounds sugar
2 teaspoons salt
1 pound currants
1 quart cider vinegar
1 pound ginger, chopped
   fine
2-3 cloves garlic,
   chopped fine
2-3 small hot peppers,
   chopped fine

1 Mix the mangoes, sugar and salt. Let stand overnight.

2 Stir and bring to a complete boil. Cook over low heat slowly until mango pieces are transparent. Stir frequently. Mix and simmer until most of liquid is taken up.

3 Combine remaining ingredients with mango mixture. Simmer for a few minutes to blend. Poor into sterile jars.

PADDY'S GRANDMA'S PICKLED PINEAPPLE

1 large pineapple, cut into
   chunks
3/4 cup pineapple juice
3/4 cup vinegar
1-1/2 cups white or 2 cups
   brown sugar
Dash of salt
8 whole cloves
3 sticks cinnamon

Delicious served with ham or chicken

1 Divide pineapple chunks into several glass canning jars.

2 Combine remaining ingredients and boil for 10 minutes. Pour over pineapple while still hot. Cover jars. Cool before storing in refrigerator.

PAPAYA SALSA

1 Combine papaya with other ingredients; stir well.

3 cups peeled, diced ripe papaya
3/4 cup peeled, diced kiwi fruit
2 tablespoons chopped red bell pepper
1-1/2 tablespoons chopped shallots
1-1/2 tablespoons chopped cilantro
1-1/2 tablespoons lime juice

SPICY CORN SALSA

1 Separate green onion tops from bottoms. Chop bottoms to equal 1-1/3 cup, mince tops to equal 2 tablespoons. Set both aside.

2 Coat a large skillet with cooking oil and place over medium heat until hot. Add green onion bottoms, 3/4 cup tomato, corn, bell peppers, and garlic. Cover and cook over low heat 15 minutes, stirring frequently. Remove from heat; stir in green onion tops, remaining 1/4 cup tomato, lime juice, red pepper, salt and pepper. Spoon into serving bowl.

10 green onions
1-1/2 teaspoons vegetable oil
1 cup seeded, chopped unpeeled tomato, divided
1 cup corn, cut fresh from cob
1/4 cup chopped green bell pepper
1/4 cup chopped red bell pepper
1 clove garlic, minced
1 tablespoon lime juice
1/4 teaspoon ground red pepper
1/4 teaspoon salt
1/4 teaspoon black pepper

KADIE'S FAMOUS MARINADE

1-1/2 cups salad oil
3/4 cup soy sauce
1/4 cup Worcestershire
  sauce
2 tablespoons dry
  mustard
2-1/2 teaspoons salt
1-1/2 teaspoons minced
  parsley
1 tablespoon ground
  pepper
1/2 cup wine vinegar
1 clove garlic, minced
1/3 cup fresh lemon
  juice (slivers of lemon
  can also be added)

For steak, lamb kabobs, and game birds

1 Combine ingredients and stir. Soak overnight. Makes 3-1/2 cups.

TERIYAKI MARINADE

6 ounces ginger, cut
  into 2" pieces and
  smashed
10 cloves garlic,
  minced
3 cups soy sauce
2 cups brown sugar
1/3 cup honey
1/2 cup cooking sherry
  or Marsala

1 Combine all ingredients and simmer for 20 minutes, let cool. Store in jar and use as needed.

ORANGE BUTTER

Delicious with country bread

1 Blend well.

1 stick butter
1-2 teaspoons minced
  orange peel

LILIKOI BUTTER

1 Melt butter over medium heat. In a large bowl measure 4 cups sugar, add eggs, mix well. Add lilikoi juice slowly, stirring constantly. Bring to a full rolling boil still at medium heat so eggs don't coddle.

2 Cool for 5-10 minutes for desired consistency.

1-1/2 cup lilikoi purée
  (unsweetened lilikoi
  juice)
4 cups sugar
4 eggs, beaten
2 sticks butter

"BUNCH 'EM UP"

By Janice Gail

Janice Gail has been working as an artist and art instructor in Waimea since 1986, first in the paniolo country of Waimea and now in the seaside village of Laupahoehoe. Trained as an illustrator in California, she now travels about the Big Island painting and teaching. Says Janice, "It is my wish to capture, on paper or canvas, the fleeting visions of our island life, in a time that marks the beginning of great change for all of us."

BREADS

BLUEBERRY STREUSEL MUFFINS

BREAKFAST MUFFINS

COUNTRY BREAD

DILL BREAD

ONION BREAD

MOM'S BREAD IN A BOWL

NICK'S FRENCH BREAD

RASPBERRY MUFFINS

WORLD'S BEST OATMEAL SCONES

SOUR CREAM MACADAMIA NUT BREAD

MALASADAS

BLUEBERRY STREUSEL MUFFINS

Streusel Topping:
1/4 cup sugar
3 tablespoons flour
1 tablespoon butter,
  chilled and cut up
1/2 teaspoon cinnamon

Muffins:
1 cup all purpose flour
1/2 cup whole wheat
  flour
2 teaspoons baking
  powder
1/2 teaspoon baking
  soda
3/4 cup sugar
2/3 cup buttermilk
1 stick butter or
  margarine
2 large eggs
1 teaspoon vanilla
1-1/2 cups frozen,
  unthawed blueberries

1 FOR STREUSEL TOPPING: Process all ingredients in food processor (using a metal blade) for 10 seconds.

2 Preheat oven to 375 degrees. Grease 12 (1/2 cup) muffin cups;   set aside.

3 FOR MUFFINS: Use food processor to process all ingredients except blueberries. Using metal blade, process for three seconds, scrape down and process again for three seconds. Transfer batter to mixing bowl and stir in the blueberries. Fill each muffin cup 2/3 full with batter. Sprinkle each muffin with one tablespoon streusel topping. Bake in preheated oven for 25 minutes or until muffins are firm and tops are golden brown. Cool in cups for 8 - 10 minutes. Remove and serve warm.

Makes 12 muffins.

BREAKFAST MUFFINS

1 Preheat oven to 400 degrees. Grease muffin pan.

2 Combine flour, sugar, oatmeal, baking powder, baking soda and salt. Gently stir in yogurt and milk, blending just until dry ingredients are moistened. Fold in cranberries.

3 Fill muffin cups 3/4 full. Bake at 400 degrees for 18 minutes or until well browned.

Yield: 12 muffins

1-1/2 cups all purpose flour
3/4 cup sugar
1/4 cup oatmeal
2 teaspoons baking powder
1 teaspoon baking soda
1/2 teaspoon salt
2/3 cup nonfat yogurt
2/3 cup skim milk
1 cup dried cranberries (frozen or canned blueberries can be substituted)

COUNTRY BREAD

1 cup wheat berries
1 teaspoon salt
2 envelopes dry yeast
3 tablespoons brown
  sugar
2-3/4 cups warm water
  (105 F to 115 F)
5 cups bread flour
1-1/2 cups pastry flour
1-1/2 cups whole wheat
  flour
1 tablespoon salt
3 tablespoons unsalted
  butter, room
  temperature
Cornmeal
All purpose flour

1 Place berries, salt and 1-1/2 cups water in a 4 cup measure. Micro cook on high 6 minutes or until mixture comes to a boil. Stir, then micro cook on high about 9 minutes or until berries are barely tender. Let stand 10 minutes. Drain well and set aside.

2 Sprinkle yeast and sugar over 2 cups water in bowl and let stand until dissolved. Stir to blend. Let stand until foamy, about 5 - 10 minutes. Combine flours, salt and wheat berries in the bowl of heavy duty mixer fitted with dough hook. With machine on low, add yeast mixture, remaining water and butter and blend until dough is moist, almost sticky and begins to climb up the hook, about 5 minutes. Turn dough out onto lightly floured surface and knead until elastic, about 5 minutes.

3 Grease large bowl. Add dough, turning to coat entire surface. Cover with plastic wrap. Let dough rise in warm draft free area until doubled in volume, about 1 1/2 hours.

4 Dust two pie plates with cornmeal. Punch dough down. Divide and shape into 2 tight balls. Put in pie plates and cover with light towel. Let stand in warm draft free area until doubled in volume, about 45 minutes.

5 Preheat oven to 400 degrees. Cut "X" in top of dough. Dust generously with flour. Bake 20 minutes. Reduce oven temperature to 350 degrees. Bake until crust is hard and bread sounds hollow when tapped on bottom, about 30 minutes. Cool on rack.

1 Soften yeast in 1/4 cup warm water. Combine cottage cheese, sugar, minced onion, margarine, egg, dill seed, salt, and soda. Add flour a little at a time, then try to knead in another 1/4 cup. Let rise until light. Stir down and put into a 1-1/2 to 2 quart casserole. Let rise again. Bake at 350 degrees for 40-50 minutes. Remove and brush with soft butter and sprinkle lightly with salt.

1/4 cups warm water
1 package yeast
1 cup lukewarm cottage
   cheese (heated gently -
   do not allow to get hot)
2 tablespoons sugar
1 tablespoon minced
   onion (instant)
1 tablespoon margarine
1 unbeaten egg
2 teaspoons dill seed
1 teaspoon salt
1/4 teaspoon soda
2 tablespoons
   Parmesan cheese
2 tablespoons oil
1 teaspoon salt
2-1/4 cups flour

ONION BREAD

2 cups water
1 package onion soup
 (dry Lipton is good)
1 package yeast
2 tablespoons sugar
2 tablespoons
 Parmesan cheese
2 tablespoons oil
1 teaspoon salt
5 - 6 cups flour

1 Boil water and soup for 10 minutes. Add sugar, cheese, oil and salt and let cool down to lukewarm. Add yeast to 2 cups flour and sift into liquid mixture and beat (by hand) about 50 strokes. Then add rest of flour, little by little until dough is firm enough to knead. Knead about 5 minutes, adding more flour until it isn't sticky, Place in a greased bowl and let rise until double. Grease top. Punch down, divide dough in half. Roll each half between hands to form long roll and place side by side on greased cookie sheet. Cover and let rise until double (or bigger) and bake 20 minutes at 350 degrees. Brush tops with milk and bake 10 minutes longer. Place on rack to cool.

MOM'S BREAD IN A BOWL

1 Dissolve yeast in one cup of lukewarm water. Meantime, sift flour, sugar and salt in large bowl. Stir in dissolved yeast. Add just enough of second cup of water to hold dough together. Mix until you have soft dough (rather sticky). Cover with clean cloth. Set in warm spot and let rise until double, about 2 to 4 hours. When dough is high and spongy, punch down with fist and beat soundly with hand. Divide in two parts and place in two greased 6" round baking dishes (glass). Cover again and let rise until dough reaches top of dish. Now start oven at 400 degrees. Brush top with melted butter and bake one hour.

Note: *This bread can be hollowed out and used as bread bowls for soup or stew. Divide the dough into 4 parts and place in four 1-quart greased bowls; let rise and bake as directed. When cool, hollow out and reserve scooped out bread for croutons. Serve soup or stew in bread bowls, top with croutons if desired.*

*1 package quick acting
 yeast
2 cups lukewarm water
4 cups sifted all purpose
 flour
1 tablespoon sugar
2 teaspoons salt*

NICK'S FRENCH BREAD

7 cups bread flour
2-1/2 cups warm water
  (115 degrees F)
1 tablespoon dry yeast
1 tablespoon salt

1 In a heavy duty mixer, add water, yeast and salt. Then mix in flour. Mix well then knead with the mixer for 8 minutes.

2 Put dough in a greased bowl to rise until double in volume.

3 Preheat oven to 450 degrees.

4 Cut dough into 5 equal pieces and shape in long French loaves. Put loaves in a "French bread" mold and let rise again until double in volume. Slash tops of loaves with a sharp knife in long diagonal cuts and brush with a mixture of egg white and a little water.

5 Bake for 15 minutes in 450 degree oven spraying with water every 5 minutes. Turn heat down to 375 degrees and continue to bake for another 15 minutes.

RASPBERRY MUFFINS

1 Preheat oven to 400 degrees. In medium bowl mix flour, soda, salt, cinnamon and sugar. Make a well in center and stir in undrained raspberries and eggs. Thoroughly mix in oil and pecans. Spoon batter into lightly greased muffin tins. Muffin cups will be full. Batter is heavy and will not overflow. Bake 15 to 20 minutes. Cool 5 minutes before removing from pan.

Note: *Recipe can also be baked in a greased and floured 9 x 5 loaf pan at 350 degrees for one hour or until a pick inserted in center comes out clean.*

1-1/2 cup all purpose flour
1/2 teaspoon baking soda
1/2 teaspoon salt
1-1/2 teaspoons ground cinnamon
1 cup sugar
1-12 ounce package frozen unsweetened raspberries, thawed
2 eggs, well beaten
2/3 cup vegetable oil
1/2 cup pecans, chopped

WORLD'S BEST OATMEAL SCONES

1 Mix flour, baking powder, baking soda, salt and sugar together. Cut shortening and butter into flour mixture. Add oatmeal and buttermilk; stir just enough to moisten.

2 Knead on floured surface for a few moments until shaped into a ball. Flatten into a 7" round, compacting edges. Transfer onto a cookie sheet. Cut into 8 pieces as you would a pie. Brush with melted butter.

3 Bake at 375 degrees for 15 to 20 minutes until light golden brown. Serve hot with butter and jam.

1 1/2 cups flour
1 teaspoon baking powder
1/2 teaspoon baking soda
1/4 teaspoon salt
1/8 cup sugar
1/4 cup shortening
1/4 cup butter or margarine
1 cup old fashioned oatmeal (not quick)
1/3 cup buttermilk or milk

SOUR CREAM MACADAMIA NUT BREAD

6 tablespoons butter,
  cut into pieces
1-1/2 cups sugar
1 egg
1/2 cup sour cream
1/2 teaspoon orange
  extract
1-1/4 cups flour
1/2 teaspoon baking
  soda
1/2 teaspoon salt
1/2 cup macadamia
  nuts, unsalted, diced
3 tablespoons minced
  orange peel
3 tablespoons orange
  juice

1 Preheat oven to 375 degrees. Coat loaf pan with cooking spray.

2 Cream butter with sugar. Beat in egg. Stir in sour cream and orange extract. Sift flour, baking soda and salt. Blend into batter. Add nuts, orange peel and juice. Mix well. Spoon into pan. Bake until tester inserted into center of loaf comes out clean, about 45 minutes.

MALASADAS

1 In a LARGE bowl, make a well with flour and add proofed yeast, eggs and remaining ingredients. Beat thoroughly until soft and smooth. Cover bowl and allow dough to rise until doubled.

2 With a circular motion around the bowl edge, turn the dough under, allow to rise, covered until doubled.

3 Heat fat for deep frying (about 4-5 inches deep) to 375 degrees.

4 Spoon small risen dough pieces about 1 1/2" (dessert spoon full) in diameter with a spoon and scrape into fat with another spoon. Fry until golden brown and turn. Remove from fat and drain.

5 Roll in granulated sugar and serve HOT!

Note: *Multiply by 20 for 1,700 pieces or 30 for 2,500 pieces.*

Dissolve and proof:
1 package yeast
1 teaspoon sugar with
1/4 cup lukewarm
  water

6 cups flour
6 eggs, beaten until
  yellow and thick
1/2 cup sugar
1/4 cup melted butter
1 cup evaporated milk
1 cup water
1 teaspoon salt
2 teaspoons nutmeg
Juice of 1 lemon or lime

HPA CHAPEL
By Kadie Harris

Kadie Harris is a graphic designer and the creative director for *The Waimea Gazette* a community magazine in Waimea. She grew up on Oahu, and studied packaging design at the Art Center College of Design in Los Angeles. Kadie moved to Waimea in 1981 with her husband, Roger and son, Sky. An avid gourmet cook, she loves to paint and enjoys surfing.

DESSERTS

COCONUT CAKE
BANANA CAKE
MARY COVEY'S CARROT CAKE
MOCHA CHOCOLATE MOUSSE CHEESECAKE
LILIKOI CHEESECAKE
WAIMEA STRAWBERRRY PIE
LILIKOI MOUSSE CAKE
GUAVA CHIFFON PIE
KENTUCKY DERBY PIE
FRENCH UPSIDE-DOWN APPLE TART
BLITZ TORTE
ANGEL FOOD COOKIES
ANGEL PIE
ALMOND COOKIES
SCOTTISH SHORTBREAD
GRANNY'S APPLE GINGERBREAD
DATE BARS
OHELO PUDDING
NANA'S SPICED FRUIT BARS
CHOCOLATE MOUSSE
COLD GRAND MARNIER SOUFFLE
FLAN
ALMOND CUSTARD
SUN VALLEY GRANOLA
VAN'S ESCALLOPED RHUBARB

COCONUT CAKE

Cake:
3/4 cup flour (not self
* rising)*
1/2 cup sugar
1 teaspoon double
* acting baking powder*
1/4 cup vegetable oil
2 whole large eggs,
* beaten lightly*
1/4 cup water
4 large egg whites

Coconut Pastry Cream:
1-1/2 cups milk
1 vanilla bean
1/3 cup + 2 tablespoons
* all purpose flour*
4 large egg yolks
2 tablespoons sugar
1-1/4 cup heavy
* cream, well chilled*
1 cup sweetened flaked
* coconut*

1 In a small bowl, stir together the flour, sugar and baking powder. In a bowl, whisk together the oil, whole eggs and 1/4 cup water. Stir flour mixture into oil mixture until batter is smooth. With electric mixer, beat egg whites until they hold stiff peaks. Stir one fourth of them into batter and fold in remaining whites gently, but thoroughly. Pour batter into a well-buttered 9" spring form pan and bake in middle of pre-heated 350 degree oven for 20 to 30 minutes or until tester comes out clean. Remove the sides of pan, invert cake onto rack removing the bottom of the pan and let the cake cool.

2 COCONUT PASTRY CREAM: In saucepan, scald milk with vanilla bean. In a bowl, whisk together 1/3 cup sugar, flour and egg yolks. Whisk milk into yolk mixture a little at a time and whisk mixture constantly for 1 minute. Pour mixture into pan and boil, whisking constantly until it is thickened. Cool. Beat heavy cream with remaining 2 tablespoons sugar until it holds stiff peaks. Fold 1 cup of whipped cream into mixtures reserving remaining whipped cream. Fold coconut into pastry cream.

3 Cut cake horizontally into 3 layers, with a serrated knife and arrange bottom layer, cut side up on serving platter. Spread half the pastry cream on top, and top with the second layer. Repeat with third layer. Spread reserved cream on the side and top of the cake and sprinkle with the coconut.

Note: *We recommend making two cakes. It makes a higher cake. There is enough cream for both.*

BANANA CAKE

This cake has nourished many ravenous swimmers after H.P.A. meets

1 Heat oven to 350 degrees. Grease a 9 x 13 cake pan.

2 Sift dry ingredients and set aside. Cream shortening and sugar, add egg and beat well. Add salt, vanilla and mashed bananas. To this mixture add dry ingredients and sour milk alternately. Stir in raisins and/or chocolate chips and nuts. Pour batter into cake pan. (If preferred, nuts can be omitted from batter and sprinkled on top instead).

3 Bake for 40-50 minutes until golden and cooked through.

4 Speedy directions: Using liquid or melted shortening, mix first 3 ingredients in a blender or food processor. Add next 4 ingredients and mix again. Pour onto dry ingredients and mix. Add nuts and chocolate chips or raisins. Bake as above.

1/2 cup shortening
1-1/4 cup sugar (white or raw)
1 egg, large
1 tablespoon vanilla
1/4 teaspoon salt
1-1/2 - 2 bananas (1 cup), mashed
1 cup sour milk or buttermilk
2 cups flour
1-1/2 teaspoon baking powder
1/2 teaspoon baking soda
1/2 cup chopped nuts
1/2 cup raisins
1 cup chocolate chips (optional)

MARY COVEY'S CARROT CAKE

*4 large carrots - finely
  shredded
1/2 pound butter
2 cups sugar
4 eggs
1 cup walnuts, chopped
1 cup chocolate chips
1 teaspoon vanilla
2 cups flour
1/2 teaspoon baking
  soda
2 teaspoons baking
  powder
1/2 teaspoon salt*

1 Cream sugar and butter. Add eggs one at a time, beating well.

2 Toss chocolate chips and nuts with some of the flour to keep them from sinking to the bottom.

3 Add carrots, coated nuts and chips to mixture. Add vanilla and sifted flour, mix well.

4 Pour into greased and floured 9" x 9" x 2" pan. Batter will rise so pan shouldn't be more than 3/4 full.

5 Bake in preheated 375 degree oven for 30 minutes.

MOCHA CHOCOLATE MOUSSE CHEESECAKE

1 Butter sides of 10" spring form pan. Combine first 4 ingredients thoroughly. Press evenly onto bottom of pan.

2 Preheat oven to 350 degrees. Beat cream cheese until smooth, add sugar gradually, mixing until well blended.

3 Add eggs one at a time and beat at low speed until smooth.

4 Melt chocolate with whipping cream over boiling water stirring frequently until smooth. Add to cheese mixture, blending well.

5 Mix in sour cream, then cooled coffee and liqueur. Add vanilla and beat until well blended. Turn into spring form pan and bake 45 minutes, or until sides are slightly puffed (center will be a bit soft, but will firm up when chilled.) Cool cake on rack.

6 Refrigerate for at least 12 hours before serving. Remove sides of pan, garnish cheesecake with shaved chocolate.

1 cup graham cracker crumbs
1/4 cup butter
2 tablespoons sugar
1/2 teaspoon cinnamon
3-8 ounce packages of cream cheese
3/4 cup sugar
3 eggs
8 ounces semi-sweet chocolate squares
2 tablespoons whipping cream
1 cup sour cream
1/4 cup espresso coffee (cooled)
1/4 cup coffee liqueur
2 teaspoons vanilla
Shaved chocolate for garnish

LILIKOI CHEESECAKE

1 envelope unflavored
  gelatin
1/2 cup sugar
1 cup boiling lilikoi juice
  (1/2 cup concentrate plus
  water to make 1 cup)
16 ounces cream cheese
Lilikoi jello (recipe below)
1-9" graham cracker crust

Lilikoi Jello:
1/3 cup lilikoi concentrate
  sprinkled with 1-1/2
  teaspoons gelatin. Stir.
Add 2/3 cup boiling water.
Stir and cool.

1 Mix gelatin and sugar. Add boiling juice. Stir. Whip cream cheese and gradually add cooled lilikoi gelatin mixture. Chill until thickened. Whip mixture and pour into crust. Chill to set completely. Carefully pour cooled jello topping on top of cheesecake.

WAIMEA STRAWBERRY PIE

Pie Crust:
1-1/2 cup flour
3/4 teaspoon salt
1/2 cup plus 2 tablespoons
  shortening
3 tablespoons ice cold
  water

4 cups strawberries,
  washed and hulled
  (2 cups whole berries)
  (2 cups mashed berries)
1/2 cup granulated sugar
3 tablespoons cornstarch
Heavy cream, whipped

1 PIE CRUST: Combine first 3 ingredients and mix with pastry blender until small ball forms. Add ice cold water and beat quickly with a fork. Bake 10 minutes at 425 degrees or until light brown.

2 Place whole strawberries in pie shell.

3 In a saucepan, add sugar and cornstarch to mashed berries. Bring to a boil and cook until thickened. Stir to prevent scorching. Mixture should appear clear. Cool slightly and pour over berries in pie shell. Refrigerate. Top with whipped cream.

LILIKOI MOUSSE CAKE

1 Beat yolks with 1/2 cup sugar. Add water and flavorings. Sift together flour, salt and baking powder. Add to yolks. Beat whites until soft peaks form and add 1/2 cup sugar. Fold into other mixture gently. Bake in cake round for 30 minutes at 350 degrees.

2 Soften gelatin in water, add lilikoi juice. Whip cream with sugar, fold all together, then chill until set.

3 Mix cornstarch and water, then add other ingredients. Cook until thickened.

4 ASSEMBLY INSTRUCTIONS: Bake cake and cool. When cool, fill center with mousse. Freeze. Before serving, top with glaze and chill until served. This cake can be frozen for up to one month.

Sponge Cake:
5 eggs, separated
1 cup sugar
3 tablespoons water
1/2 teaspoon vanilla
  extract
1/2 teaspoon lemon
  extract
1 cup flour
1/2 teaspoon salt
2 teaspoons baking
  powder

Mousse:
1 envelope gelatin
2 tablespoons water
1/2 cup lilikoi juice
  (fresh, unsweetened)
5 tablespoons sugar
1 cup whipping cream

Glaze:
2 tablespoons water
1/4 cup lilikoi juice
2 tablespoons sugar
1/2 teaspoon cornstarch

GUAVA CHIFFON PIE

6 ounces frozen guava
  concentrate
1 tablespoon
  unflavored gelatin
1/4 cup water
4 eggs, separated
1/4 cup lemon juice
2 tablespoons sugar
Few drops of red food
  coloring
1/4 teaspoon salt
1/2 cup sugar
1 baked 9" pie shell
8 ounces whipping
  cream, whipped

1 Thaw guava juice. Soften gelatin in water. Beat egg yolks well. In a saucepan, combine beaten yolks, lemon juice and 2 tablespoons sugar. Cook over low heat, stirring constantly until mixture thickens. Stir in gelatin and remove from heat. Cool slightly. Stir in guava juice and food coloring. Chill until mixture begins to thicken. In a small bowl, beat egg whites with salt until soft peaks form. Gradually beat in 1/2 cup sugar. Fold into guava mixture. Pour into pie shell and chill until firm. Top with whipped cream before serving. Enjoy!

KENTUCKY DERBY PIE

2 eggs, slightly beaten
1 cup sugar
1/2 cup flour
1 stick butter, melted
  and cooled
1/2 cup chopped
  pecans
1 cup chocolate chips
1 teaspoon vanilla

1 Combine ingredients in order given, stirring after each addition and mixing well.

2 Spread in 9" unbaked pie shell. Bake at 350 degrees for 35 minutes. If frozen crust is used bake at 325 degrees for 1 hour.

3 Remove from oven, let pie set up.

4 Serve warm, topped with vanilla ice cream or whipped cream.

FRENCH UPSIDE-DOWN APPLE TART

1 Preheat oven to 425 degrees. Peel, core, and thickly slice apples. In 9 inch tart pan, make a caramel with 2 tablespons of butter and half of the sugar. Arrange apple slices in pan and sprinkle with remaining sugar. Cut remaining butter into small pieces and dot over apples. Roll out pastry to 1/4 inch thick and cut out an 11 inch round. Place pastry round over apples and press edges down.

2 Bake in oven for 30 minutes. Turn tart out of pan immediately with caramelized apples on top. Can be served with creme fraiche or vanilla ice cream.

1 lb. firm apples,
  Golden Delicous or
  Granny Smith
1/2 cup butter
3/4 cup sugar

Basic Short Pastry:
4 ounces softened
  unsalted butter
8 ounces sifted flour
Water
1/2 tablespoon sugar
Pinch of salt

BLITZ TORTE

1/2 cup shortening
1 teaspoon vanilla
1/2 cup sugar
3 tablespoons milk
1/8 teaspoon salt
1 cup cake flour, sifted
4 egg yolks, lightly
  beaten
1 teaspoon baking
  powder

Topping:
4 egg whites
3/4 cup sugar
1/2 cup sliced, blanched
  almonds
1 teaspoon sugar
1/2 teaspoon cinnamon

Filling:
1/3 cup sugar
3 tablespoons
  cornstarch
1/4 teaspoon salt
2 egg yolks
2 tablespoons butter
2 cups milk, scalded
1 teaspoon vanilla

1 Cream shortening, beat in sugar and salt. Add egg yolks, vanilla, milk and flour (sifted with baking powder). Spread mixture in 2 round greased cake pans.

2 Beat egg whites until very light. Add 3/4 cup sugar gradually and spread on unbaked mixture in both pans. Sprinkle with almonds, 1 teaspoon sugar and cinnamon. Bake in moderate oven (300 degrees) about 30 minutes. Cool. Put together with cream filling. Makes one 9" two layer cake.

3 FOR THE FILLING: Combine sugar, cornstarch, salt and egg yolks. Beat thoroughly. Add butter and enough milk to make a smooth paste. Add paste to remaining hot milk and cook over boiling water, stirring constantly until mixture is thickened. Cool and add vanilla. If desired, add 1/2 cup chopped nuts to mixture.

ANGEL FOOD COOKIES

1 Mix dates, nuts and flour. Beat egg whites, salt and cream of tartar until soft peaks form; gradually beat in sugar until stiff.

2 Fold in vanilla and lemon extract, then fold in dates and nuts.

3 Drop by heaping teaspoon onto greased sheets.

4 Bake in 350 degree oven for 10-12 minutes.

1 cup dates, snipped
1 cup pecans or
  walnuts, chopped
1 cup flour
3 egg whites
Pinch of salt
Pinch of cream of
  tartar
1 cup sugar
1/2 teaspoon vanilla
1/2 teaspoon lemon
  extract

ANGEL PIE

1 Sift together 1 cup of the sugar and the cream of tartar. Beat the egg whites until stiff, but not dry. Gradually add sugar mixture and beat until thoroughly mixed. Line a 9"-10" greased pie plate with this mixture, being careful not to get too close to the rim. Bake at 275 degrees for 1 hour. Cool.

2 Beat the egg yolks slightly. Add remaining 1/2 cup sugar, lemon juice and rind. Cook in top of double boiler until very thick (8-10 minutes). Remove and cool. Whip cream. Combine half of the cream with lemon-egg mixture. Fill pie shell. Cover with remaining cream. Chill in refrigerator overnight.

1-1/2 cup sugar
1/4 teaspoon cream of
  tartar
4 eggs, separated
3 tablespoons lemon
  juice
1 tablespoon lemon
  rind, finely grated
1 pint heavy cream

ALMOND COOKIES

1/2 cup butter
1/2 cup margarine
1 cup sugar
1 cup vegetable oil
1 teaspoon almond
  extract
4 - 4 1/2 cups white
  flour
1 teaspoon baking soda
1/2 teaspoon salt

1 Cream together butter, margarine and sugar. Add vegetable oil and almond extract and mix well.

2 Combine dry ingredients. Add dry mixture to above.

3 Roll into balls, place on an ungreased cookie sheet and flatten with thumb. Dip the round tip of a chopstick in red dye and mark cookie in the center.

4 Bake for 15-20 minutes at 350 degrees. Do not brown too much.

SCOTTISH SHORTBREAD

2 cups flour - unsifted
1/3 cup powdered sugar
1/2 pound butter

1 Sift flour and powdered sugar together onto a pastry cloth. Place butter in center of cloth. Knead into dry ingredients. Pastry will look rather flaky, but keep kneading.

2 Form into ball. Roll out 1/4 inch thick. Cut out with cookie cutter. Place on cookie sheet. Bake in 350 degree oven for 15 minutes or until brown around the edges. Remove, cool, and put into airtight tins.

GRANNY'S APPLE GINGERBREAD

Granny Calder served this in her tearoom in Portland, Oregon during the 1920s.

1 Before you start mixing the batter, peel, core and slice apples into the buttered cake pan in which you intend to bake the dessert. Add enough sugar to sweeten and a little water to start the syrup or juice. Cook in the oven while you are mixing the batter.

2 For batter, mix sugar, molasses and egg. Combine soda, baking powder and spices with flour. Add to sugar mixture. Add water last. Pour batter over cooked apples and bake 30-40 minutes at 325 degrees. Test with a straw or toothpick.

3 Serve with whipped cream and a sprinkle of cinnamon.

5 or 6 apples
1/2 cup butter (scant)
1/3 cup sugar
1/3 cup molasses
1 egg, beaten
1-1/4 cup flour
1 teaspoon baking soda
1/2 teaspoon baking powder
1/2 teaspoon cinnamon
1/2 teaspoon cloves
1 teaspoon ginger
Pinch of salt
1/2 cup hot water

DATE BARS

1 pound chopped dates
1 teaspoon baking soda
1 cup boiling water (1/2
  cup boiling water and
  1/2 cup Kona coffee
  may be substituted)
1 cup butter
1 cup sugar
2 eggs
Dash of salt
1-3/4 to 2 cups flour
2 teaspoons cocoa
6 ounces chocolate
  chips
1 cup nuts, chopped
2 tablespoons sugar

1 Mix baking soda and hot water, pour over dates.

2 Cream butter and sugar. Add eggs one at a time and mix thoroughly. Stir in dates.

3 Sift together salt, flour and cocoa and add to wet mixture.

4 Pour batter into oiled 9 x 13 pan. Combine 6 ounces chocolate chips and nuts with 2 tablespoons sugar. Sprinkle over top of cake. Bake at 350 degrees for 45 minutes (325 degrees if glass pan is used). A bundt pan may be used if desired.

OHELO PUDDING

1 quart ohelo berries,
  washed
1 cup sugar
3 tablespoons
  cornstarch
1/8 teaspoon salt
  (optional)
1 cup water
1 tablespoon butter

1 Mix 1 cup berries in pan with sugar, cornstarch, salt and water. Cook, stirring, over low heat until thickened. Add uncooked berries and butter. Mix well and cool.

2 Serve with ice cream, whipped cream or yogurt.

NANA'S SPICED FRUIT BARS

Great for the holidays!

1 Place raisins, sugar, hot water and butter in saucepan and bring to boil for 4 minutes. Pour into mixture of flour, soda, cinnamon, nutmeg, cloves and salt. Mix until blended and pour into well-greased pan (10-1/2" x 15 1/2").

2 Bake at 350 degrees for 20 minutes. Have glaze ready to pour on top when taken from oven.

3 Mix powdered sugar, vanilla and lemon juice to "running" consistency.

2 cups raisins
2 cups sugar
2 cups hot water
1 cup butter
4 cups flour
2 teaspoons baking
  soda
2 teaspoons cinnamon
1 teaspoon nutmeg
1 teaspoon cloves
1 teaspoon salt

Glaze:
1/2 box powdered
  sugar
1 teaspoon vanilla
1/4-1/2 cup lemon
  juice

CHOCOLATE MOUSSE

*1 envelope unflavored
  gelatin
2 tablespoons sugar
1-1/2 cups milk
6 ounces chocolate
  chips, semi-sweet
1 teaspoon vanilla
1-1/2 cups whipped
  topping*

1 In medium saucepan, mix gelatin, sugar, and milk. Let sit 1 minute. Stir over low heat until gelatin is dissolved.

2 Add chocolate chips. Continue cooking until the chocolate is melted. Whip with whisk to blend. Add vanilla.

3 Pour in large bowl, chill, stirring occasionally, until mixture mounds slightly when dropped from spoon. Fold in whipped topping.

4 Chill until set. Garnish if desired with chocolate shavings or strawberries.

COLD GRAND MARNIER SOUFFLE

1 Whisk together egg yolks and sugar in top of double boiler over barely simmering hot water. Continue whisking vigorously until mixture thickens and there are no sugar grains.

2 Stir gelatin mixture and add to custard. Whisk over heat until gelatin is dissolved (2 minutes). Add Grand Marnier and let bowl cool in refrigerator to room temperature. Beat egg whites until stiff and whipping cream in separate bowls. When custard is cool, fold egg whites and custard by thirds, into whipped cream.

3 While custard is cooling, make collar of wax paper for 1 quart souffle dish and butter. Coat with granulated sugar. Pour souffle into dish and chill at least 4 hours.

Quick tip: *Custard can also be cooled by putting bowl into another bowl filled with ice cubes and stirred.*
If desired, any liqueur such as Ameretto or Cointreau, may be substituted for Grand Marnier.

5 large eggs, separated
2/3 cup white sugar
1 envelope gelatin, softened in 1/4 cup cold water
1/3 cup Grand Marnier
1 cup heavy cream, whipped

FLAN

1-3/4 cups sugar
6 eggs
4 cups milk
1 1/2 teaspoon vanilla

1 Caramelize 3/4 cup sugar. Pour into 3 quart shallow casserole. In large mixing bowl, beat eggs, gradually adding remaining 1 cup sugar. Heat milk over medium until it bubbles. Slowly add milk to egg mixture. Stir in vanilla.

2 Pour egg mixture into casserole. Place casserole in a baking pan on oven rack. Pour hottest tap water into baking pan to the depth of 1 inch. Bake uncovered for 40 minutes at 325 degrees.

3 For 6 servings, halve the recipe and bake in an 8 inch round pan for 30-35 minutes.

ALMOND CUSTARD

1 envelope unflavored
   gelatin
1/4 cup + 2 tablespoons
   water
1-1/4 cup vanilla
   nonfat yogurt
1/2 cup sugar
1/2 cup frozen egg
   substitute
1/2 teaspoon almond
   extract
2 tablespoons chopped
   almonds

1 Sprinkle gelatin over water and let sit 1 minute. Cook over low heat until dissolved.

2 Combine yogurt with remaining ingredients (using Cuisinart or electric mixer). Slowly add gelatin. Mix until well blended. Pour into custard cups. Chill until set. Sprinkle with almonds before serving.

Note: *Strawberry nonfat yogurt can be substituted for vanilla yogurt. Use vanilla extract instead of almond and top with strawberries. About 135 calories per 1/2 cup.*

SUN VALLEY GRANOLA

This is a great gift or can be put into zip-lock bags and mailed to children away at school.

1 Heat oil, honey and vanilla in large saucepan. Remove from heat. Add remaining ingredients and mix well. Spread in 13 x 9 baking pan. Bake at 350 degrees for 15-20 minutes or until golden. Cool. Makes about 8 cups of granola.

1/2 cup vegetable oil, butter or margarine
1/2 cup honey or maple syrup
1 teaspoon vanilla
2 cups rolled oats (quick or old fashioned)
2 cups whole wheat cereal flakes
1 cup sunflower seeds
1 cup raisins
1/2 cup walnuts, chopped
1/2 cup coconut, flaked

VAN'S ESCALLOPED RHUBARB

1 Melt butter in pan with food coloring. Add bread crumbs to pan until coated, add sugar and rhubarb. Place in greased pan or casserole. Add 1 teaspoon water in each corner if fresh rhubarb is used. Bake 45 minutes at 325 degrees.

Note: *Can also serve as vegetable accompaniment with lamb or poultry.*

3 cups cubed bread (crisp in oven)
3 cups diced rhubarb
1 cup sugar
1 cube butter, melted (don't substitute)
1 teaspoon red food coloring

INDEX

INDEX

- -

THANK YOU FOR SUPPORTING HAWAII PREPARATORY ACADEMY

KAMAKANI COOKS

KAMAKANI COOKS
c/o H.P.A. Parents Assoc.
P.O.Box 428
Kamuela, Hawaii
96743

Please send _____ copies   @ $14.95 each _____
Shipping and Handling   @ $ 3.50 each _____
Outside the U.S. Shipping   @ $ 5.50 each _____
TOTAL ENCLOSED $_____
Please make Checks payable to H.P.A. Parents Assoc.

NAME: _____

ADRESS: _____ CITY: _____

STATE: _____ ZIP: _____

- -

THANK YOU FOR SUPPORTING HAWAII PREPARATORY ACADEMY

KAMAKANI COOKS

KAMAKANI COOKS
c/o H.P.A. Parents Assoc.
P.O.Box 428
Kamuela, Hawaii
96743

Please send _____ copies   @ $14.95 each _____
Shipping and Handling   @ $ 3.50 each _____
Outside the U.S. Shipping   @ $ 5.50 each _____
TOTAL ENCLOSED $_____
Please make Checks payable to H.P.A. Parents Assoc.

NAME: _____

ADRESS: _____ CITY: _____

STATE: _____ ZIP: _____

- -

THANK YOU FOR SUPPORTING HAWAII PREPARATORY ACADEMY

KAMAKANI COOKS

KAMAKANI COOKS
c/o H.P.A. Parents Assoc.
P.O.Box 428
Kamuela, Hawaii
96743

Please send _____ copies   @ $14.95 each _____
Shipping and Handling   @ $ 3.50 each _____
Outside the U.S. Shipping   @ $ 5.50 each _____
TOTAL ENCLOSED $_____
Please make Checks payable to H.P.A. Parents Assoc.

NAME: _____

ADRESS: _____ CITY: _____

STATE: _____ ZIP: _____

- -